Icelandic Constitutional Reform

This collection documents, analyses, and reflects on the Icelandic constitutional reform between 2009 and 2017. It offers a unique insight into this process by providing first-hand accounts of its different stages and core issues. Its 12 substantive chapters are written by the main actors in the reform, including the Chair of the Constitutional Council that drafted the 2011 Proposal for a New Constitution.

Part I opens with an address by the President of the Republic and positions the constitutional reform in its full complexity and longer-term perspective, going beyond the frequent portrayal of that process in international discussion as being solely a result of the 2008 financial crisis. Part II offers a nuanced and contextualised reflection on Iceland's innovative approach to consultation and drafting involving lay participants, including its twenty-first-century digital take on 'the people,' which attracted international attention as 'crowdsourcing.' Part III analyses the main constitutional amendment proposals, and focuses on natural resources and environmental protection, which lie at the heart of Iceland's identity. The final part reflects on the reform's wider significance and includes an interview with the current Prime Minister, who is now taking the reform forward.

The volume provides a basis for reflection on a groundbreaking constitutional reform in a democratic context. This long and complex process has challenged and transformed the ways in which constitutional change can be approached, and the collection is an invitation to discuss further the practical and theoretical dimensions of Iceland's experience and their far-reaching implications.

Ágúst Þór Árnason (1954–2019) was one of the leading figures of Icelandic constitutionalism. He taught at the University of Akureyri, where he contributed to setting up the Law School, and founded the Polar Law Programme in 2008 with Professor Guðmundur Alfreðsson. He was directly involved in the initial stage of the constitutional reform process as a member of the 2010–2011 Constitutional Commission.

Catherine Dupré is Associate Professor of Comparative Constitutional Law at the University of Exeter. She has studied the processes of constitutional change and reform in Hungary (post-communism and since 2010) and in the UK since 1998. She has been following Icelandic constitutional developments since 2008 when she first visited the University of Akureyri as a guest lecturer. She is the author of *Importing the Law in Post-Communist Transitions: The Hungarian Constitutional Court and the Right to Human Dignity* (Hart Publishing 2003) and of *The Age of Dignity: Human Rights and Constitutionalism in Europe* (Hart Publishing 2015).

Comparative Constitutional Change

Comparative Constitutional Change has developed into a distinct field of constitutional law. It encompasses the study of constitutions through the way they change and covers a wide scope of topics and methodologies. Books in this series include work on developments in the functions of the constitution, the organization of powers and the protection of rights, as well as research that focuses on formal amendment rules and the relation between constituent and constituted power. The series includes comparative approaches along with books that focus on single jurisdictions and brings together research monographs and edited collections which allow the expression of different schools of thought. While the focus is primarily on law; where relevant, the series may also include political science, historical, philosophical, and empirical approaches that explore constitutional change.

Series editors:

Xenophon Contiades is Professor of Public Law, Panteion University, Athens, Greece, and Managing Director, Centre for European Constitutional Law, Athens, Greece.

Thomas Fleiner is Emeritus Professor of Law at the University of Fribourg, Switzerland. He teaches and researches in the areas of Federalism, Rule of Law, Multicultural State; Comparative Administrative and Constitutional Law; Political Theory and Philosophy; Swiss Constitutional and Administrative Law; and Legislative Drafting. He has published widely in these and related areas.

Alkmene Fotiadou is Research Associate at the Centre for European Constitutional Law, Athens.

Richard Albert is Professor of Law at the University of Texas at Austin.

Also in the series:

Rule of Law, Common Values and Illiberal Constitutionalism
Poland and Hungary within the European Union
Edited by Tímea Drinóczi and Agnieszka Bien-Kacała

Icelandic Constitutional Reform
People, Processes, Politics
Edited by Ágúst Þór Árnason and Catherine Dupré

For more information about this series, please visit: www.routledge.com/Comparative-Constitutional-Change/book-series/COMPCONST

8 The 2011 Proposal for a New Constitution

Analysis and critical comments

Skúli Magnússon

Introduction

The present Constitution of the Republic of Iceland was enacted by the Althing (the Icelandic Parliament) in 1944 after being approved by 95.04% of the votes in a national referendum in which 98.61% of the electorate participated. Although 'new,' the Constitution was to a large extent based on the Constitution of the Kingdom of Iceland of 1920, the first constitution enacted after Iceland was recognised as a sovereign state in 1918. The 1920 Constitution was modelled on the very first concise Icelandic Constitution, 'offered'[1] by King Christian IX in 1874 which, in turn, was largely based on the first Danish Constitution of 1849 as amended in 1866.[2] The Danish Constitution of 1849, having as one of its main models the Constitution of Belgium of 1830, signified the end of absolutism by conferring legislative and fiscal powers to an elected Assembly and providing for the protection of fundamental rights, much in line with the 1789 French Declaration of the Rights of Man and the Citizen. This background places the current Constitution of Iceland within the general trend of European constitutionalism.

With no consensus on a fully fledged constitutional reform during the preparations for creating a Republic during the Second World War, it had been decided in Iceland, as early as 1942, to put political disagreement aside and limit the revision to those constitutional amendments necessary for a full separation from the Danish Monarchy and the creation of a Republic. It followed that the substantive

1 Considering that Iceland was only in (a personal) union with the Danish State through a common sovereign (the King), Icelanders were generally firmly against adopting the Danish Constitution of 1849 which they saw as equalling an annexation to the Danish State. After having repeatedly rejected Danish proposals, which provided for a certain degree of autonomy but not full independence, the Althing approved a proposal in 1873 for an Icelandic Constitution. However, the Althing also asked the King to 'give' the country a constitution in case the proposal would be rejected, which was highly likely! It was upon this request and on the basis of his sovereign powers as an absolute monarch over Iceland, that the King ended the constitutional deadlock by issuing the 1874 Constitution.

2 The most important amendments to the 1874 Constitution were the creation of the 'Home Rule' in 1903 (effective from 1904) and changes to the electoral system in 1915 which inter alia provided for women's right to vote.

amendments in 1944 were essentially limited to the form of government, replacing the King with a President, to be directly elected by the People. A full revision of the Constitution was foreseen once external conditions had improved after the war. Thus, it was indeed foreseen that the Icelandic People would make 'their own' Constitution in due time. Nevertheless, it remains open to debate to what extent the makers of the 1944 document envisaged an entirely 'fresh start' whereby even the most basic elements of the constitutional order would be up for revision.[3] As discussed in this chapter, however, in many ways that turned out to be the outcome of the revision process initiated in 2010.

Whatever may have been expected in 1944, what followed in the post-war era proved to be more akin to 'patch-working,' whereby only some, albeit important sections of the Constitution were revised.[4] Furthermore, during this period, discussion on constitutional issues was mainly limited to political and academic circles without much interest or involvement by the public. This scenario radically changed in the aftermath of the meltdown of Iceland's financial sector in autumn 2008[5] – characterised by economic crisis, political turmoil, and widespread distrust in state institutions, combined with an acute demand for political reforms, inter alia through the making of a new constitution.

This chapter analyses the outcome of the revision process launched by Act 90/2010 creating a Constitutional Assembly, intended to satisfy public expectations for reforms through a new constitution. At the forefront is the 2011 Proposal for a New Constitution (CP) delivered by the Constitutional Council in July 2011. It is noted that the (formal) Bill for a new Constitution submitted to the Althing on 16 November 2012, by the government, contained some technical refinements but was in terms of substance intended to be identical to the CP.[6] Hence, unless otherwise indicated, reference is made to the 2011 Proposal. The analysis is critical inasmuch as it is argued that the substantive constitutional order intended to emerge from the CP in many respects conformed poorly with the stated aims of the Council as well as with some established values of constitutionalism. This chapter focusses on the political and institutional system envisaged by the CP and contains

3 Contemporary sources suggest that this revision was going to be focussed on rather limited issues, e.g. the electoral system and the organisation of the (then bicameral) Althing, rather than changing the very core of the Constitution. See e.g.: Speech by Bjarni Benediktsson (1908–1970) on 21 January 1953 published in *Morgunblaðið* 22–24 January 1953 under the heading 'On the Revision of the Constitution.'

4 The constitutional basis for the electoral system was revised two times, in 1959 and again in 1999. In 1991, provisions relating to the Althing were revised with the aim of strengthening the Parliament vis-à-vis the Cabinet and abolishing the existing bicameral system. In 1995, a new chapter on fundamental rights was enacted with the chief aim of harmonising these rights with European and international human rights law. All in all, the Constitution was amended seven times from 1944 to 1999.

5 See: Chapter 4 by Kristrún Heimisdóttir in this collection.

6 For a full text of the Proposal and some explanatory remarks in English, see the webpage of the Constitutional Council: www.stjornlagarad.is. The full Commentary (skýringum) on the Proposal is, however, only available in Icelandic. All webpages last accessed on 2 June 2020.

only a brief discussion on the CP's Chapter II on Fundamental Rights and Nature, leaving aside issues dealt with elsewhere in this collection, such as natural resources[7] and environmental protection.[8] At the outset, it is necessary, however, to give some account of the events constituting the background and substance of Act 90/2010 which provided the legal basis for the CP.

Crisis or constitutional moment?

A new constitution, perceived as a key element in enhancing fundamental political and social changes, sometimes referred to as the ideal of 'New Iceland,' was a common theme in the numerous protests during the winter of 2008–2009.[9] It was in this extraordinary social context that it was recalled that the People had been 'promised' a new Constitution in 1944. The fact that the 'establishment' never seemed to have delivered on this promise fitted nicely with the widespread distrust in public institutions, in particular the Althing and the government.[10] Furthermore, it followed from this view that a constitutional project could not be entrusted to the decayed institutions of the '*ancien régime*' and should in one way or another be conducted directly by the People. However, this demand for a 'hands-off approach' also extended to academics and experts, in particular lawyers.[11] The elections of April 2009, conferring a clear majority on the left-wing government (already in place since February), gave such a radical approach towards constitutional reforms an impetus.[12] In fact, the left-wing government had already on 4 March, viz. before renewing its mandate in the elections, made a proposal whereby a Constitutional

7 See: Chapter 10 by Ragnheiður Elfa Þorsteindóttir in this collection.

8 See: Chapter 11 by Aðalheiður Jóhannsdóttir in this collection.

9 In a press announcement by Voices of the People (Raddir fólksins), probably the most influential of various popular movements emerging in autumn 2008, it is stated that the 'will of the Icelandic People is to rebuild the Republic by writing a new Constitution and changing the rules of politics.' It further reads: 'Let us emphasise on building a new Iceland, a new Republic and a new Nation' (www.visir.is on 22.01.2009). Other, albeit less prominent popular movements, carried names referring to a similar ideal, e.g. 'New Times,' 'New Iceland,' and 'New Republic.' This manifesto was, by and large, taken up by a new political party supported by various popular movements in the beginning of 2009, the Citizens' Movement, which won four seats in the elections of spring 2009 and proved to be an ardent supporter of the 2011 Proposal and the 2012 Constitutional Bill submitted to the Althing.

10 For further reading on the 'spirit' of the protests, see Jón Gunnar Bernburg and Anna Soffía Víkingsdóttir, 'Political Opportunity, Framing, and Mobilization in Iceland's Post-Crash Protests' in Valur Ingimundarson, Philippe Urfalino, and Irma Erlingsdóttir (eds), *Iceland's Financial Crisis: The Politics of Blame, Protest and Reconstruction* (Routledge 2016) 81–103.

11 Thorvaldur Gylfason, one of the members of the Constitutional Council, states that '[l]egal expertise, even if it can be helpful, is not really essential to writing a constitution, because the constitution superseeds ordinary legislation by virtue of the fact that the people are superior to Parliament': 'Constitution on Ice,' in Valur Ingimundarson, Philippe Urfalino, and Irma Erlingsdóttir (eds) (n 10) 203, 204.

12 The cabinet consisted of a coalition of the Left-Green Movement and Social Democrats supported by the Citizens' Movement.

Assembly would be elected to draft a new constitution, conferring only an advisory role upon the Althing.[13]

Against this background, the reinstated government, now enjoying a parliamentary majority, made a full revision of the Constitution by an independent democratic body one of its priorities, a goal ardently supported by a new party emerging from the popular movements of autumn 2008, the Citizens' Movement (*Borgarahreyfingin*). Consequently, a Bill, initially submitted by PM Jóhanna Sigurðardóttir in July 2009, was finally passed after lengthy negotiations with the opposition in June 2010, as Act 90/2010 for the Creation of a Constitutional Assembly (*lög nr. 90/2010 um stjórnlagaþing*).

Legal basis and aims of the drafting process

In contrast to the first proposal of the government of 4 March 2009, Act 90/2010 was not to affect the formal amendment procedure provided for under Article 79 of the Constitution.[14] However, limited attention was given to the political role of the Althing, once the Constitutional Assembly (whose functions were later assumed by the Constitutional Council) had delivered its Proposal.[15] Hence, views were split, even within the Constitutional Council itself as it turned out, on whether the Althing had, in political terms, 'outsourced' its role and in any case whether the Althing was permitted to do so under the current Constitution.[16]

Under Article 3 of Act 90/2010, the Assembly was, 'in particular' (sérstaklega), to address eight issues, including the organisation of the legislature and the executive as well as the limits of the powers of these branches; the function

13 *Proceedings of the 136th Legislative Assembly* 2008–2009, Doc. No 648–Case 385.

14 Pursuant to Article 79(1) of the current Constitution, constitutional amendments are enacted by two subsequent and independently elected Althings. It follows from this two-round system that if a constitutional amendment is approved in the first round, the Althing is to be dissolved, new elections are to take place, and the newly elected Althing will have to approve the amendment for the second round. The Constitution of 1944 was, however, enacted on an ad hoc constitutional basis (established in 1942 under the two-round system) whereby a bill for a new constitution could be agreed by the Althing and submitted to a national referendum for final approval.

15 As explained by Jón Ólafsson, 'The Constituent Assembly' in Valur Ingimundarson, Philippe Urfalino, and Irma Erlingsdóttir (eds) (n 10) 252–272. The members of the Council, by and large, considered the Althing morally obliged to follow the CP, once delivered. This, however, was clearly not the view of the political opposition in the Althing, in particular the centre-right Independence Party (Sjálfstæðisflokkkur). The preparartory materials were vague on the matter, stating that 'although the result of the Constitutional Assembly being consultative and not binding, it is beyond doubt that a Bill of the Council must have essential political importance, in particular if based on a consensus.' See: *Proceeding of the 138th Legislative Assembly* 2009–2010, Doc. No 168–Case 152.

16 As discussed by Salvör Nordal, the Chair of the Constitutional Council, this ambiguity quite possibly affected the workings of the Council ('Constitutional Revision – A Weak Legislative Framework Compounded by Political Disputes' in Valur Ingimundarson, Philippe Urfalino, and Irma Erlingsdóttir (eds) (n 10) 220–229. For further discussion in this collection, see also Chapter 7 by Jón Ólafsson.

and status of the President of the Republic; and 'the democratic participation of the public, the timing and organisation of referenda, inter alia on constitutional matters.' However, it was expressly stated that the Assembly could also decide to deal with any 'further issues' (*fleiri þætti*). The Council would later use this open-ended clause to propose quite dramatic amendments, such as the reformulation of provisions on fundamental rights and changes to the constitutional basis of the Church of Iceland.

In line with the 'hands-off' approach underscoring the 2010 Act, the Explanatory Notes to the Bill did not contain guidelines on the substantive part of the revision.[17] Thus, the substance was to be left to the discretion of the Constitutional Assembly. However, the Explanatory Notes made it clear that the process envisaged by the Act was exceptional and not in any way intended to become the standard for future constitutional revisions. Describing the nature of the process, a reference was made to historical precedents, such as the United States in 1787, Germany in 1949, and South Africa in 1996. It was further noted that Constitutional Assemblies 'typically mark the beginning of a new State or new Governance in the aftermath of war, revolution or break-down of the community order and resulting constitutional crisis.' In addition, reference was made to the Constitution as the manifestation of 'the social contract.' Therefore, the making of such social contract should be (directly) with the People as the supreme and ultimate holder of the constituent power.[18]

The Constitutional Council's aims and ideology[19]

The choice of full revision

Given the limited time frame, the groundwork made by the Constitutional Commission, also established by the Act 90/2010, and the relative functionality of the existing constitutional framework, it might perhaps have been expected that the Constitutional Council would only use its 'carte blanche' cautiously.[20] True enough, the Commentary

17 Explanatory Notes (greinargerðir) to legislative bills are official documents considered to constitute important guidance for legal interpretation under Icelandic law, much in the same way as would be the case in other Nordic legal systems. They are sometimes also referred to as preparatory materials to legislation. In practice, the use of these materials generally means that the actual legal text is kept relatively short and detailed explanations left to the Explanatory Notes.

18 See: *Proceeding of the 138th Legislative Assembly* 2009–2010, Doc. No 168–Case 152.

19 As will be recalled, the Supreme Court of Iceland annulled the elections to the Constitutional Assembly by a decision on 25 January 2011. The persons elected were subsequently appointed to a Constitutional Council by the Althing by Resolution of 24 March 2011. Since the Resolution corresponded to Act 90/2010 on the Creation of a Constitutional Assembly, this event is peripheral to subject matter of this chapter.

20 The Constitutional Commission (stjórnlaganefnd) was set up on the basis of the 'interim provision' of Act 90/2010 creating the Constitutional Assembly. See also: Chapter 5 by Björg Thorarensen in this collection.

accompanying the CP contained various references to the existing Constitution as well as the 2011 Report assembled by the Constitutional Commission which inter alia contained two draft proposals for a new constitution. However, even where it was stated that the CP contained provisions equivalent or comparable to existing ones, the wording had in many cases been reformulated with the aim of rewriting the text in the 'language of the ordinary man' (*stjórnarskráin á mannamáli*). More importantly, the CP provided for major changes to all major institutions of the State as well as their interrelations. These changes were magnified by a new electoral system and provisions on citizens' initiative and national referendum.

In its Commentary on the CP, the Council referred to three basic values as its guiding light: separation of powers, transparency, and responsibility. As to the first of those three, reference was made to a more thorough separation among the three branches of the State as well as increased public participation in decision-making, or 'direct democracy.' In particular, the Commentary referred to the intention of drawing a clearer line between the legislature and the executive while also conferring more powers on the parliamentary opposition. It was also underlined that the CP was generally intended to improve the rights of citizens against the authorities, inter alia by emphasising transparency and the public's right to information.

As to substance, the Commentary highlighted a new Chapter II on Fundamental Rights and Nature, whereby existing rights would be enhanced inter alia with more detailed and 'modernised' formulation of existing provisions. Furthermore, reference was made to entirely new provisions, e.g. a specific provision on the freedom of the press and on the protection of the environment and natural resources. As to the legislative and executive branches, the Commentary mentioned several amendments intended to improve the legislative function of the Althing as well as its budgetary role and powers to keep the administration under scrutiny. It was further explained that by subjecting the election of the Speaker of the Althing to a qualified majority vote (two-thirds of votes cast), the position of the political opposition would be strengthened with the intention of enhancing the dialogue between the parliamentary majority and minority.

As to the goal of promoting 'direct democracy,' the Council's Commentary referred to various new provisions, inter alia the right of 10% of the electorate to have legislation put to a referendum and the right of 2% to put any matter on the agenda of the Althing. A wholly new election system based on equality of votes, and individual selection of candidates was to be put in place (as opposed to mainly choosing between political parties under current legislation).

With regard to the executive branch, the Commentary mentioned a turn towards 'affirmative parliamentarianism,' whereby the Althing would elect the PM, who henceforth could be voted out of office only if the majority of the Althing had agreed on his or her successor. Among other reforms intended to draw a clearer distinction between the Alþhing and the government, the Commentary mentioned provisions prohibiting members of Althing to serve simultaneously as ministers. The Cabinet Meeting (*ríkisstjórnarfundur*) was also to become a formal administrative body where all major decisions would be taken by a majority vote of ministers (instead of the Cabinet being chiefly a political forum for consultation and harmonisation of ministers). Finally, the Commentary made note of reformed provisions relating to the judiciary, a new chapter on foreign affairs, and the strengthening of local government. Several of these new provisions are discussed in more detail next.

Drafting from scratch

Given the impressive list of issues mentioned by the Constitutional Council in its Commentary, the numerous and sometimes radical reforms proposed, as well as the reformulation of almost any provisions taken from the current Constitution, the CP was clearly intended to constitute a runway for profound political and social changes, very much in the spirit of the so-called 'pots and pans revolution' (*búsáhaldabyltinging*) and the ideal of 'New Iceland.' Accordingly, the document was, by and large, characterised by an attempt to draft a 'new Constitution from scratch,' albeit drawing on existing provisions in some cases.

The radical character of the CP – as well as the method of reformulating any existing provision made use of in the 'language of the ordinary man' – were bound to make it susceptible to certain technical criticism, e.g. with regard to the use of legal concepts, precision of provisions, etc. These flaws would, however, to some extent be repaired by a Working Group of Legal Experts, appointed by the Althing in June 2012 and entrusted to prepare a document to be submitted as a (formal) Bill for a new constitution of Iceland.[21] Accordingly, this Bill was presented by the government in the Althing on 16 November that year.[22] In spite of these refinements, the Venice Commission – requested by the Althing to assess the pending Bill in November 2012 – concluded 'that numerous provisions of the Bill have been formulated in too vague and broad terms, which, despite the clarifications that might be provided by the preparatory materials to the Bill, may lead to serious difficulties of interpretation and application, including in the context of the adoption of the implementing laws.'[23]

Critical comments on the CP's key features

The CP consisted of a Preamble and 114 articles, organised in nine chapters, accompanied by a Commentary, all of which would be impossible to discuss in detail here. Hence, the following discussion is not so much concerned with the text of specific provisions of the CP but is rather focussed on the main features of the

21 Reference is made to the conclusions of the Working Group in its letter to the Constitutional and Supervisory Committee of the Althing of 12 November 2012: www.althingi.is/pdf/skilabref_fylgiskjol.pdf

22 *Proceeding of the 141th Legislative Assembly* 2012–2013, Doc. No 510–Case 415. To be exact, the Bill was submitted to the Althing by the majority of the Constitutional and Supervisory Committee of the House but ardently supported by PM Jóhanna Sigurðardóttir.

23 'Opinion on the Draft New Constitution of Iceland Adopted by the Venice Commission at its 94th Plenary Session', Venice, 8–9 March 2013, p. 31: https://www.venice.coe.int/webforms/documents/?pdf=CDL-AD(2013)010-e

material constitution likely to emerge from the document. The aim of this section is to compare these elements with some of the principal aims of the Constitutional Council itself and, in some cases, to discuss them further with regard to the basic values of European constitutionalism, such as predictability, stability, and division of powers.

Strengthening parliamentarianism?

One of the explicit aims of the Council was to strengthen parliamentarian rule by reinforcing the Althing in particular vis-à-vis the government. Thus, Article 1 of the CP described the form of government as 'Republican with Parliamentarian Rule.' Furthermore, under Article 37, the supremacy of the Althing with regard to legislative and fiscal powers, as well as the monitoring of the executive branch, was affirmed. Other provisions were also intended to safeguard the independence of members of the Althing in particular vis-à-vis the government, e.g. the election of the Speaker of the House by a qualified majority vote (CP Article 52). In addition, under Article 62 CP, an independent advisory body of experts (Lögrétta) was to assist the Althing in assessing the constitutionality of legislative bills as well as their compliance with international obligations.

However, various other elements of the CP gave rise to concerns with regard to the general aim of strengthening the position of the Althing and parliamentarian rule. Firstly, the new electoral system in CP's Chapter III was expressly intended to weaken party control and to encourage more individualised politics. Irrespective of the far-reaching effects on political parties and the working of democracy, it had therefore to be expected that *the Althing would become more fragmented*, with its majority depending on the issue at hand rather than on party lines or participation of parties in government.

Moreover, pursuant to CP Article 90, the Althing was now to elect the PM upon nomination by the President of the Republic while the PM would consequently appoint other ministers (who could not be members of Althing). The PM could be voted out of office only by the Althing once there was a majority on his or her successor (CP Article 91). However, given the new character of the Althing (in particular in view of the election system proposed), it could be foreseen that members of the parliament would have difficulties in reaching any agreement on a successor. As a result, it seemed quite possible that a PM would not be replaced despite having in fact lost majority support. In my view, this equalled a risk of a stalemate situation where a government would continue in office without the capacity of getting anything through the Althing. Furthermore, this called into question not only the value of effective government but also the very principle of parliamentary rule.

The involvement of the President of the Republic in forming the government also implied a new and more direct role of the President with the possible developments towards a 'French-style' presidency. Thus, the President might be active in negotiating the next PM with members of the Althing with the result of becoming politically responsible for the Cabinet and government policies. However, such a turn towards a strengthened semi-presidential system contradicted the aim of strengthening parliamentarianism as well as the stated aim of the CP to limit the President's powers and political engagement.

Finally, the position of the Althing was potentially weakened not only vis-à-vis the government but also with regard to influence by popular initiatives discussed further later in the chapter. Thus, the increased possibilities for the public to have legislation put to national referendums or to have matters put directly on the agenda of the Althing were likely to encourage MPs to work with actors external to the Althing and conventional party politics, such as interest groups, labour unions, popular movements, or even commercial companies. This concern was only aggravated by the envisaged election system, which would also encourage politicians to reach beyond party politics. Indeed, these elements of the CP raised the question whether the drafters of the CP perceived the role of the new and reformed Althing as a 'listener to the voice of the People,' rather than operating independently on the basis of a democratic mandate in line with representative democracy. If such a turn was the latent intention of the Council, the CP demonstrates the difficulties in reconciling 'direct democracy' with the aim of truly strengthening parliamentarian rule.

The role of the President of the Republic

The current Constitution confers vast powers upon the President of the Republic, but in real terms most of these powers are executed by the government. An important exception to this is the President's power to suspend any legislation enacted by the Althing and to refer it to a national referendum (Article 26 of the current Constitution). After three such decisions and two referendums in 2010 and 2011, concerning Acts implementing so-called Icesave Agreements with the UK and the Netherlands, these presidential powers are no longer called into question.[24] Another substantial role of the President consists of his or her responsibilities in forming a new government after parliamentary elections.

Furthermore, the President's signature (together with a countersignature of the Minister in charge) is also required for all major decisions by the executive, e.g. the ratification of international agreements, the dissolution of the Althing and the

24 Although Article 26, concerning the President's limited power of veto was among the very few entirely new provisions of the 1944 Constitution, it was nevertheless argued, mainly by politicians in the post-war era but also by certain academics, that the President could not make use of this provision without the support of his or her ministers. According to this theory, the position of the President was equal to the position of the Danish Monarch, as it had evolved throughout the twentieth century, depriving the Sovereign of any real powers. In 2004, however, President Ólafur Ragnar Grímsson refused to sign a much debated Act on Media referring to his powers under Article 26. The Government reacted to this by having the Act revoked by the Althing thus avoiding a national referendum. Although no referendum took place, this conclusion nevertheless signified that the President's personal power to suspend legislation could no longer be ignored, as the referendums in 2010 and 2011 would later confirm. For further discussion in this collection, see Chapter 3 by Ágúst Þór Árnason and Catherine Dupré.

appointment of Supreme Court judges, to give only some examples (Article 19, 21, and 24 of the current Constitution). These powers are considered mainly formal inasmuch as the President will, as a rule, follow a proposal by the Minister in charge (which, in turn, is endorsed or tolerated by parliamentary majority). Nevertheless, there have been exceptional cases where the President refused a proposal made by a Minister or signed one only after due consideration and a statement of his or her own reasons.[25]

According to the current Constitution, the collaboration of the President and Ministers takes place in the State Council (*ríkisráð* – not to be confused with Cabinet Meetings which are headed by the PM). Although in practice the President will usually sign legislation and acts of government between formal meetings of the Council, the State Council is the formal forum of interaction between the President and the Ministers. The very existence of the Council also reflects the constitutional principle that *the supreme executive power of the State is vested jointly in Ministers* (each independently responsible and accountable before the Althing) *and the President* (as Head of State and elected directly by the People).

Arriving at the remarkable conclusion that the State Council was an obsolete and pointless institution, the Constitutional Council envisaged it to be entirely abolished! Thus, the Commentary on the CP described the President's role under the current system as one of a 'patch' (*leppshlutverk*), i.e. having only a purely formal function. Now, while this view of the Council may hold for the vast majority of government matters submitted to the President, it very much ignores the possibility of exceptional situations and more generally the function of the President as a 'safety valve' in the constitution. It also falls short of taking into account the possible tacit influence of the President on the workings of government and the Althing.

With regard to the powers of the President vis-à-vis the Althing, the CP contained various amendments aimed at reducing presidential powers. Firstly, the President was no longer to be defined as part of the legislative branch (CP Article 2).[26] This meant that the confirmation of Acts of the Althing by signing them (or refusal to confirm) was now considered an executive (or administrative) decision, not as participation in the legislative process. In case of refusal to sign, the President was also henceforth to be required to state reasons for his or her decision to refuse (CP Article 60). This raised the question whether this decision of the President could be reviewed through judicial proceedings such as would be the rule for any

25 To give some examples, President Ólafur Ragnar Grímsson refused to dissolve the Althing and call for new elections at the request of PM Sigmundur Davíð Gunnlaugsson in spring 2016. In summer 2017, President Guðni Th. Jóhannesson appointed 15 judges to the newly established Court of Appeal (*Landsréttur*), at the request of the Minister of Justice, but only after conducting his own inquiry into the matter and concluding that no manifest mistakes had been made in the appointment procedure.

26 Article 2 of the current Constitution vests the legislative power in the Althing and the President jointly. Hence, the President's confirmation of an Act of the Althing – or refusal to confirm – has been considered application of his or her legislative powers rather than an executive act.

administrative decisions under Icelandic law. The CP also granted the Althing the explicit competence to withdraw any Act in the face of a refusal by the President, thereby relieving the parliament (and/or the government supporting the act in question) of the prospect of being 'voted down' by the People in a subsequent national referendum.

Finally, as is the case under Art 11(4) of the current Constitution, the Althing would continue to have the power to remove the President by a three-quarter majority, pending a national referendum. However, under the CP, this would now be without the parliament risking being dissolved and new elections taking place in the case of an unfavourable outcome in the referendums. This, again, was also apt to weaken the position of the President in the event of a clash with the Althing.

The reduced role of the President with regard to national referendums envisaged by the CP was due to the view that it was more democratic to have referendums based on citizens' initiative under Article 65 of the CP rather than a decision by 'one person.' However, unlike the CP's provisions on national referenda upon citizens' initiative (discussed later in the chapter), the present Article 26 gives the President an unqualified right to refer any legislation to a national referendum. In this respect, the system of national referenda set up by the CP as further discussed below was considerably weaker than the current one under Article 26.

Given the relatively weak position of the President envisaged by the CP, the Venice Commission in its Opinion expressed doubts as to whether direct elections were at all appropriate for this office. According to the Venice Commission, an election by a larger panel of local and national politicians might have been a possible option as opposed to general presidential elections.[27] In any case, the Venice Commission considered that 'a more adequate balance could have been found between the direct election of the President and the scope of the presidential powers.'[28] This was, however, leaving aside the enhanced powers of the President with regard to the formation of government, previously discussed, which could, in factual terms, constitute a step towards a semi-presidential system. To sum up, the CP aimed to reduce the role of the President in some respects while, rather confusingly, conferring new powers on the office in others.

Splitting up the executive branch

In line with the abolition of the State Council, individual ministers, appointed by the PM, were now, as a rule, to sign executive acts on their own without having to seek the confirmation (i.e. the countersignature) of the President of the Republic

27 It is remarked that the Venice Commission pays, in this respect, no attention to (or is perhaps ignorant of) the historical background of the office of the President of Iceland. The initial proposal for a new constitution in 1943 did indeed envisage the President being elected by the Althing. It was only under pressure that the Althing yielded to a popular demand for having the President directly elected by the People. It is submitted that a proposition for not having the President directly elected by the People would still be deeply upsetting for many Icelanders.

28 Venice Commission Opinion (n 23) 15–16.

(cf. Article 19 of the current Constitution). In formal terms, this arrangement constituted a fundamental change whereby Ministers, acting wholly independently, were now defined as the highest agents of the Executive branch (CP Article 2 and 86.1). However, this fundamental change to the position of Minister was blurred by adopting a 'Swedish-style' arrangement whereby the Ministers were to take all important decisions collectively by a majority vote in the Cabinet (CP Article 87.3). Hence the Cabinet, acting collectively, was also listed among the highest agents of Executive power (CP Article 2). The President was also to continue to be involved in a limited number of ministerial decisions pursuant to certain provisions of the CP. Some of these provisions, e.g. concerning the appointment of the Supreme Court judges and the State Prosecutor, made it clear that the President could actually refuse a proposal submitted by a Minister, in which case the matter should be referred to the Althing for a decision by a qualified majority of two-thirds (CP Article 96.3). In such a situation, it would therefore seem that the Althing was to take decisions pertaining to the Executive branch without any involvement by a responsible Minister.[29]

All in all, the structure of the Executive branch set out by the CP looked complicated compared to the simplicity (at least in formal terms) of the 1944 Constitution.[30] With no unity of the Executive, the role of the President and ministerial responsibility would therefore have to be assessed on a case-by-case basis. These complications were perhaps best summarised by the cautious wording of the Venice Commission, who stated in its 2013 Opinion that 'the government organisation should be carefully reconsidered with a view to achieving a more unified and coherent system.'[31]

Implications of direct democracy

As discussed, under Article 26 of the current Constitution, the President may expressly refuse to confirm an Act passed by the Althing and refer it to a national referendum for a final decision on its validity.[32] The current Constitution provides for referendums under two further situations: if the Althing decides to remove the

29 I.e. it would seem that in this case a power of executive nature was vested in the Althing.

30 The principle of political responsibility and accountability of Ministers before the Althing is partially based on express provisions in the current Constitution (cf. in particular Article 54 on the right of MPs to request information or ask Ministers questions) and partially based on custom (cf. the obligation of a Minister to resign in event of a vote of no-confidence in the Althing), as well as statutory law. The civil and criminal liability of Ministers is based on Article 14 of the Constitution and further implemented by law.

31 Venice Commission Opinion (n 23) 19.

32 When the Althing approves a bill, the bill becomes 'Law by the Althing' (lög frá Alþingi). However, for the law to come into force, the President of the Republic must confirm the Act in question, together with the Minister in charge. However, if the President refuses to confirm the Act, as was e.g. the case in 2010 and 2011 with regard to the Icesave legislation, the Act will nevertheless enter into force pending the outcome of a national referendum, cf. Article 26 of the current Constitution. This qualified power to veto was intended to prevent the President from being able to block legislation by the Althing, even temporarily, but it has the obvious downside of creating uncertainty during the period between the President's decision and the national referendum on the validity of the legislation.

President (Article11.3) and if the National Church of Iceland is to be abolished or reformed (Article 79.2). Referendums have also sometimes taken place pursuant to specific Acts of the Althing, such as the referendum on the Constitution and the formation of a Republic in 1944. However, popular initiatives, whereby the President of the Republic was called upon to use his or her powers under Article 26, have in most cases been unsuccessful, the most famous example being the accession of Iceland to the European Economic Area in 1993.[33] It follows that Article 26 of the current Constitution has by many been found to be insufficient as the appropriate tool for resolving potential conflicts between the Althing and the People on polemic issues.

As noted, CP was based on the idea that the presidential powers under Article 26 of the current Constitution should more and less be replaced by public initiatives. This view also sat well with the aim of increased public participation in the government and the ideal of direct democracy emphasised by the pots and pans revolution. Accordingly, the CP provided for public participation in the following cases:

1 Referendum upon the President's refusal to confirm parliamentary legislation (CP Article 60.2)
2 Referendum upon a petition of 10% of the electorate for the annulment of parliamentary legislation (CP Article 65)
3 Initiation of parliamentary work upon a proposal endorsed by 2% of the electorate (CP Article 66.1)
4 Initiative for a bill of law or any other parliamentary act endorsed by 10% of the electorate with subsequent national referendum on the proposal (CP Article 66.2)
5 Referendum concerning a decision by the Althing to remove the President (CP Article 84.2)
6 Referendum on a decision by the Althing to transfer powers, allocated by the Constitution, to an international organisation (CP Article 111.3)
7 Referendum on constitutional amendments (CP Article 113)

Turning first to CP Article 66 (initiation of parliamentary work upon a proposal endorsed by 2% of the electorate), the first paragraph entailed no obligation for the Althing to proceed in any special way with an item put on its agenda by the citizens pursuant to this provision. In my view, this provision therefore added next to nothing to an (informal) ordinary citizens' petition to the Althing to take up a certain matter. In addition, this provision was unclear as to its procedural

33 Faced with a petition, endorsed by a formidable portion of the Icelandic People, to refer the question of accession to the European Economic Area to a national referendum in January 1993, President Vigdís Finnbogadóttir signed Act 2/1993, implementing the Agreement. However, she did so only after submitting a written statement in the State Council in which she explained that such an involvement in the decision-making process of the democratically elected Althing would be an unprecedented move on behalf of the President.

implications. For instance, who was to prepare and present the matter in the Althing? Under CP Article 66.2 (initiative for a bill of law or any other parliamentary act endorsed by 10% of the electorate with subsequent national referendum), this popular initiative was also considerably weakened by leaving it to the Althing to decide whether a subsequent referendum would be binding. Both provisions reflected the general intent to reinforce the public vis-à-vis the Althing but were hardly likely to bring about much concrete changes.

As to the modus operandi of the national referendum referred to in Article 65 (referendum upon a petition of 10% of the electorate for the annulment of parliamentary legislation) as well as the referendums referred to under Article 66 (sections 1 and 2), further criteria were specified in CP Article 67 which required that any matter to be put to a referendum should 'concern the public interest' but, more importantly, excluded the State budget, fiscal matters, citizenship, as well as any laws entailing implementation of international obligations. It was further provided that it would be for the courts to rule on possible disputes concerning the interpretation and application of these criteria. However, neither the CP itself nor the accompanying Commentary, gave further directions as to how such cases should be processed or assessed by the courts. It may be noted that Icelandic courts have typically been reluctant to engage in the assessment of evaluative constitutional criteria, such as 'public interest,' and have therefore given the authorities a considerable margin of discretion in this respect. Concerns about the discretionary nature of these criteria were also echoed by the Venice Commission which stated in its 2013 Opinion that they entailed 'the risk of litigation and legal uncertainty as well as a great responsibility for the bills' drafters when it comes to ensuring that the bills of popular initiative are consistent with the Constitution.'[34]

From the viewpoint of constitutional democracy, it was more worrying that CP Article 67 contained no participation threshold for potential national referendums. Hence it could not be excluded that a relatively small but determined, faction of the electorate could both push for a referendum, e.g. under Article 65, and be highly influential in determining its outcome.[35] Apart from the obvious risk of creating a platform for rising populism, the prospect of having legislation, already in force for several months, retrospectively annulled by a referendum also raised questions with regard to legal certainty and possible liability of the State vis-à-vis those relying on the legislation while in force. Lastly, there was perhaps also reason for a more general concern with regard to the overall efficiency of the legislative process given the various channels of public initiatives.

In spite of the Council's proclaimed dedication to increased public participation in the political process, the Commentary on the CP made it clear that 'direct democracy' was considered only a supplement to representative democracy rather than constituting its essence.[36] In line with this, CP Article 1 referred only to

34 Venice Commission Opinion (n 23) 22.

35 In Iceland, 10% of the electorate equals only ca. 25,000 persons.

36 Commentary (n 6) 106.

Parliamentary Rule without mentioning the 'People' or referring otherwise explicitly to direct democracy as one of the Republic's foundations. The Commentary also stipulated that the Constitutional Council was aware of certain risks relating to direct democracy, such as the danger of decision-making becoming ineffective, the possibility of abusive decisions against minorities, and the potential decline of political responsibility by MPs.

In my view, the CP provisions on public participation, when taken as a whole, seemed likely to undermine the foundations of representative democracy and the position of the Althing, in particular when also taking into account the proposed changes to the electoral system previously discussed. Although paying allegiance to representative democracy, the heart of the Constitutional Council therefore seemed in many respects to beat with the ideals of direct democracy creating an inconsistent framework for political decision-making. Thus, in spite of its stated aims, the CP begged the question as to what concept of democracy provided its rationale.

Voicing similar concerns, the Venice Commission stated in its Opinion that 'direct democracy mechanisms may considerably influence politics and the political equilibrium within the country and have a significant impact in terms of political stability and the actual capability of the institutions to govern efficiently.' Accordingly, the Venice Commission (highly) recommended a 'more cautious approach towards such mechanisms and a thorough review of the relevant provisions, based on a careful impact assessment, both from a legal and political perspective.'[37]

Foreseeability, stability, and the Rule of Law

In its Opinion of 2013, the Venice Commission described the institutional system set out by the Proposal as 'rather complex and marked by lack of consistency.' The Commission further affirmed that:

> [t]his concerns both the powers granted to each of the main constitutional actors – parliament, government and President – the balance between them and their inter-institutional relations, often too complicated, as well as the mechanisms of direct participation introduced by the Bill.[38]

Personally, I would submit that the Constitutional Council did not have a clear and concise vision on how the substantive constitution emerging from its document was supposed to operate in a way that would satisfy basic requirements of constitutionalism. Thus, the capital defect of the CP was the lack in *foreseeability*

37 Venice Commission Opinion (n 23) 15.

38 Ibid. (n 23) 31. It is recalled that the Opinion of the Venice Commission concerned the 2012 Bill for a new Constitution submitted to the Althing in autumn 2012. Since the Bill was based on the CP of 2011, only with some technical amendments, the Opinion applies a fortiori to the CP.

as to its material constitution. But apart from this, there was also reason to doubt that several of the stated aims of the Council would, in fact, be achieved with the adoption of the CP. For instance, in spite of its stipulated aims, the CP was, on a closer reading, not likely to enhance a strong parliamentary regime but rather to create a weak fragmented legislative assembly susceptible to pressure from various directions, including the government or private interest groups.

Furthermore, given the complex institutional structure envisaged, the CP risked creating a power vacuum where different agencies of State could try to take advantage of legal gaps and compete for more influence. This concern was in particular relevant to the largely unwritten role of the President of the Republic and his or her relations to the government and the Althing. However, the CP's provisions pertaining to parliamentary elections were also complicated and unclear on a variety of issues, leaving further implementation and clarifications to the legislature (CP Article 30). Hence, the functioning of the Althing and its capability to act as a check on the government was difficult to predict.

Finally, there were also concerns as to the *stability* of the new constitution. In particular, the provision on constitutional amendments made it possible to have any parts of the Constitution, including fundamental rights, amended at any time by a simple majority of the Althing together with a simple majority of voters in a national referendum without any quorum (CP Article 113). Given the heated debate about several issues of substance in the CP, it could therefore be expected that the Constitution, or at least certain sections of it, would become a common item on the agenda of any political movement. This equalled the Constitution becoming the object rather than the basis of day-to-day politics.

Reformulating fundamental rights

The Fundamental Rights chapter of the current Constitution was thoroughly revised in 1995 with the general aim of aligning these provisions with the European Convention on Human Rights and other international instruments. There is little doubt that this was the main reason why Act 90/2010 on the creation of a Constitutional Assembly did not list fundamental rights among the issues to be addressed in the revision process. Nevertheless, the Council decided to give this part of the current Constitution a thorough revision. However well intended this might have been, the new fundamental rights provisions were not without problems.

Firstly, the reformulation of existing provisions by using 'the language of the ordinary man', although sometimes without any overt intention of making changes to the substance, ignored the truism that when dealing with established constitutional provisions, even a small change to the wording may raise new issues of interpretation and give rise to legal challenges. To take one example, CP Article 6 declares 'us all equal before the law' in a comparable way to Article 65 of the current Constitution, which declares 'all *to be* equal before the law.' Furthermore, both provisions refer to differential treatment as discrimination when it is based on certain grounds, such as sex, religion, opinions, ethnic origin, race, colour, economy, family, and position. However, the CP added new elements to this list, such as sexual orientation, disability, political connections, language, domicile, family and genetic make-up, thereby creating a source for a variety of difficult legal questions and hard cases for the courts.[39]

Secondly, the Constitutional Council sometimes seemed to lack full understanding of the legal context in question. One example was the reformulation of the existing provision for the protection of private property in CP Article 13. Thus, the Council decided to cut from the existing provision a sentence stating that property rights of foreign individuals or companies in respect of land (real estate) can be limited by law, explaining in its Commentary that this provision was contrary to the principle of equality and international obligations of the State. In my view, that premise is entirely unsubstantiated.

Thirdly, in some cases the formulation of new provisions generated more questions than they answered. One example is CP Article 112 concerning the standing of international law relating to fundamental rights and the environment. In its Commentary, the Council argued that it had not been possible to give international rules any direct effect since that would have equalled 'not only the transfer of power [to international bodies] to legislate but also the power to amend the Constitution as such.'[40] Nevertheless, the wording of CP Article 112(1), obliging any agent of the State to respect international human rights law binding upon the State, could very well be interpreted as providing for the direct effect of these rules.[41] Moreover, CP Article 112(2) gave the Althing the authority to transpose international treaties on fundamental rights and environment by statutes 'which should henceforth take priority against any general statutes.' This provision, however, was unclear as to whether the primacy of these statutes, transposing international rules, was based only on the established interpretative principle of presumption or on a new constitutional rule of primacy.[42]

Finally, some provisions the Constitutional Council attempted to settle issues, once and for all, that have been debated in Icelandic politics for decades. Thus, CP Article 34 stipulates that private parties can be given permits for exploiting natural

39 The 'equality provision' in Article 65 of the current Constitution has, since its enactement in 1995, been the basis of various legal actions concerning the constitutionality of allocating individual transferable quotas in fisheries, reduction of disability allowances due to the income of a spouse or partner, various rights of disabled persons, the determination of damages for physical impairment for women, only to name few examples. It is noted that at the time of its drafting, Article 65 was considered to constitute only the codification of principles already inherent to the Constitution. The inference to be drawn from case law is, however, that the provision had vast and largely unforeseen effects.

40 Commentary (n 6) 197.

41 I discuss this provision of the CP in detail in a paper published in Icelandic: 'Er þörf á stjórnarskrárákvæði um stöðu þjóðaréttar' [On the Necessity of a Constitutional Provision on the Status of International Law], published in Svala Ísfeld Ólafsdóttir (ed), *Fullveldi í 99 ár – Safn ritgerða til heiðurs dr. Davíð Þór Björgvinssyni sextugum* [*Sovereignty for 99 – A Collection of Essays Honouring Dr. Davíð Thor Björgvinsson*] (The Icelandic Literary Society 2017) 143–167.

42 I.e. the established principle that the legislature is presumed to respect international obligations when enacting any domestic laws which should, in turn, be interpreted in line with any rules of international law binding upon the State.

resources only against a 'full price' (*gegn fullu gjaldi*).[43] This equalled taking the issue of regulating fees for the exploitation of natural resources off the agenda of ordinary politics and placing it within the framework of a constitutional provision. It could therefore be expected that the judiciary would be drawn into one of the most controversial political issues in Iceland during the past decades and would be required to interpret 'full price,' in particular with regard to the allocation of exploitation permits in the fisheries and energy sectors. However, the attempt to take this out of the realm of ordinary politics was very likely to backfire inasmuch as it could be foreseen that several Icelandic political parties would work to have this provision amended as soon as possible. This, again, raised the question whether this issue was not better left to general elections, ordinary politics, and decisions by the Althing as the general legislature.

Leaving behind these critical comments, it should be stressed that many of the ideas put forward by the Council for reformed fundamental rights were sound and, without doubt, all of them were well intended. However, the overall picture emerging from the various new provisions on fundamental rights was too tainted by uncertainty and instability. It is submitted that, given the narrow time frame and the resources available to it, the Council was simply too ambitious in its attempt to give these complex issues a complete revision. Before submitting the Bill for a New Constitution on 16 November 2012, some of the technical defects of this part of the CP were addressed and repaired by the Working Group of Legal Experts previously referred to. Nevertheless, the Venice Commission concluded in its Opinion (on the 2012 Bill) that provisions pertaining to fundamental rights needed generally 'increased precision and substantiation as to the scope and nature of the protected rights and related obligations.'[44]

Concluding remarks: a missed opportunity?

The link between constitutional shortcomings and the financial crisis of autumn 2008 were, from the outset, a disputed issue. True enough, there was a virtual consensus on the need for a more or less global revision of the Constitution, inter alia in light of issues brought forward by the crisis. However, this consensus was arguably not tantamount to the view that the crisis constituted any sort of 'constitutional moment,' justifying rewriting the current Constitution from scratch in an attempt to create a 'New Iceland.' As a result, the radical approach adopted by the Constitutional Council in drafting its Proposal in 2011 was bound to become controversial and meet opposition. This risk was only enhanced by the fact that the current Constitution, although admittedly flawed in some respects, had proved to be a sufficient basis for major political changes in the aftermath of the crisis and that these changes had, in turn, triggered various actions aimed to deal with the

43 This is further discussed by Ragnheiður Elfa Þorsteinsdóttir in Chapter 10 in this collection.

44 Venice Commission Opinion (n 23) 31. Fundamental rights are further discussed in this collection by Björg Thorarensen (Chapter 5).

causes and consequences of the events of autumn 2008. Only to name a couple, these actions included the establishment of a Special Prosecutor for Financial Crimes and the indictment of PM Geir H. Haarde by the Althing before the State Court in autumn 2010.

The aims set out by the Council were generally sound and in line with the established values of European constitutionalism. The good intentions and hard work of all those involved in the Council are equally beyond question. Furthermore, a lot could be said about the deficiencies of the legal basis of the process, the insufficient time frame, and resources. Irrespective of these problems (for which the Council was, of course, not to blame), it is the main conclusion of this chapter that the Council was, above all, overambitious in the number of reforms and novelties proposed. Some of these reforms were alien to Icelandic constitutional law, e.g. the introduction of affirmative parliamentarianism and the idea of making the Cabinet an administrative body. Other reforms were directed towards undisputed and unproblematic aspects of the Constitution, e.g. the existence of the State Council, relations between the President of the Republic and Ministers, and the formation of a new government.

Considering the CP as a whole, it is difficult to figure out the likely operation of the system that would have resulted from the Proposal. Attempting to rewrite provisions of the current Constitution in the 'language of the ordinary man' (sometimes without the intention of amending the substance of existing provisions) only added to this problem. Most seriously, the CP gave rise to concern as to the stability and efficiency of the new constitutional order. Thus, in its Opinion of January 2013, the Venice Commission stated that overall 'there are reasons [. . .] to see the risk of political blockage and instability, which may seriously undermine the country's good governance.'[45] As reflected by this conclusion, approving the Constitutional Bill of 2012 (in spite of the technical refinements it contained compared to the original CP) would have constituted a leap of faith – a move difficult to justify in a society with a functioning Constitution.

Although the crisis of autumn 2008 may, arguably, not have amounted to a 'constitutional moment' for a 'failed State,' it nevertheless represented an important opportunity for a global revision of the current Constitution – a project that undeniably has been on the agenda since 1944 and not properly addressed by the several 'patching-ups' during the post-war era.[46] With a more careful and moderate approach, the Constitutional Council could, in my opinion, have produced a

45 Ibid.

46 An attempt for a global revision of the Icelandic Constitution was made directly after the creation of the Republic in 1944 under the auspices of a Constitutional Committee of the Althing. It faded out in the fifties without any formal proposal being submitted to the Althing. A new attempt was made in the seventies, during which the Constitutional Committee set up did not reach a consensus on a global proposal. However, one member of the Committee, Gunnar Thoroddsen, being Prime Minister at the time, submitted his own proposal for a new constitution in 1983 based on the Committee's work. A new process for a concise revision was initiated in 2003 which was still ongoing in autumn of 2008 when constitutional matters took a different turn. It is noted that the work done by these committees produced in some cases limited amendments to the Constitution.

document addressing the flaws and gaps of the current Constitution (as mapped by academic work and earlier reports, inter alia the extensive Report of the 2011 Constitutional Commission), as well as adding important reforms of its own, in particular provisions relating to citizens' initiatives and new principles relating to transparency and integrity. In my view, the Council should also have left the chapter on fundamental rights, revised in 1995, mostly untouched. The same applies to the constitutional basis for the Church of Iceland which is an issue that merits its own debate and is, as such, to be subject to a separate referendum under the current Constitution. Furthermore, a more cautious approach with regard to other heavily debated matters, such as the functions of the President of the Republic, would have been justified in the light of the limited time frame and resources allocated to the Council's work. Lastly, I believe that there is reason to think that the Council's scepticism towards the input of legal experts (although perhaps not entirely unwarranted!) played at least some part in the unsuccessful outcome.[47]

Judging from the present situation, as well as the proceedings and the outcome of three parliamentary elections – in 2013, 2016, and 2017 – the 'Constitutional Project' seems, once again, to have lost much of its momentum by becoming a relatively low-ranking item on the agenda of the present government. Public debate on the Constitution has, sadly, become more and more polarised, with one side arguing that the CP should be adopted as a new Constitution, more or less unchanged, and the other side more or less defending a status quo, i.e. fighting against any changes.[48] There seem to be relatively few advocates for a middle ground solution, whereby a concise constitutional revision would take place, albeit placing emphasis on addressing gaps and shortcomings of the Constitution in a disciplined manner without turning the present system upside down and taking a leap of faith into constitutional uncertainty.

In this sense, the fate of the CP (and the 2012 Bill) represents a missed opportunity for those genuinely interested in taking steps towards a revised Icelandic Constitution, based on constitutional democracy, fundamental rights, and the rule of law. It is hoped that the CP, with its numerous innovations, will nevertheless serve as a source of ideas and reference for any future revision. It is also hoped that it will serve as a vivid reminder of the fact that the project innate to the Constitution of 1944 – to make a proper Constitution for the Republic of Iceland – still remains to be carried out.

47 I criticise the legal expert advice referred to by the Constitutional Council underpinning the formulation of CP Article 112 in Magnússon (n 41), 159–161. Thus, the Commentary on the CP states that the Council supported the idea of giving international human rights treaties direct effect on a constitutional basis but was advised against it by constitutional expert since this would equal 'not only transferring legislative powers to a foreign body but also the power to make constitutional amendments' (n 6) 197.

48 The Constitutional Committee working from 2013 to 2016 delivered proposals for only three new provisions without ever getting into other issues: (1) protection of the environment; (2) natural resources; (3) national referendums upon public initiative. These are discussed in Chapter 9 by Páll Þórhallsson. A bill based on these proposals was submitted to the Althing by PM Sigurður Ingi Jóhannsson without much enthusiasm and without being submitted to a final vote before the dissolution of the Althing. A new constitutional committee was appointed after the change of Government in autumn 2017, and it remains to be seen whether it will deliver anything.

9 The 2016 Bill of the Constitutional Committee

Three proposals for reforming the 1944 Constitution

Páll Þórhallsson

Introduction

In the mind of many Icelanders, the most important milestone in the long process to gain independence from Denmark was the establishment of the Republic in 1944. However, inter alia because of time pressure, the crafting of a totally new constitution was not feasible in 1944. The existing constitution of 1920, primarily a translation of the Danish constitution, was adapted to new circumstances as the King had to be replaced with the President. The Parliamentary Committee, which prepared the necessary constitutional changes in 1944, was subsequently tasked with continuing its work. A new committee established in 1947 was also supposed to propose a new constitution.[1] That committee failed in its endeavour, and the same can be said of all later attempts to revise the constitution as a whole. This does not mean that no changes at all have been made since 1944. There have been piecemeal reforms, most notably the revision of the human rights chapter in 1995.[2] Still, for many, the sentiment remains that we do not have a truly Icelandic Constitution.

Following the economic crisis in 2008, the constitutional question was again put forcefully on the political agenda. The 2009–2013 government, led by Social Democrat Jóhanna Sigurðardóttir, made it one of its priorities to fulfil the promise of wholescale revision.[3] A huge effort was made, and a Constitutional Council of 25 laypeople drafted a Proposal for a New Constitution in 2011,[4] supported in an advisory referendum held on 20 October 2012.[5] The slim majority in parliament at that time was not

1 Parliamentary Resolution of 14 May 1947.

2 Act 97/1995. Following the incorparation into Icelandic law of the European Convention on Human Rights in 1994, it was deemed necessary to update the human rights chapter of the Constitution. Otherwise, Courts would have had great difficulty in enforcing human rights on the basis of simple legislation.

3 Government programme of 8 May 2009: www.stjornarradid.is/media/stjornarrad-media/media/Skjol/rikisstjorn_8mai09.pdf (all webpages last accessed 1 June 2020).

4 See: Chapter 6 by Salvör Nordal and Chapter 8 by Skúli Magnússon in this collection.

5 The referendum was controversial. The parliamentary majority decided to hold it to boost a struggling proposal (Parliamentary Resolution no. 37/140 of 24 May 2012). However, the main question put to voters was ambiguous ('Do you want the proposal of the Constitutional Council to form the basis of a bill for a new constitution?').

able to push the 2012 constitutional bill through before the end of its term in April 2013. Instead, a temporary constitutional provision was adopted, allowing constitutional revision through an extraordinary procedure involving Parliament's approval with an increased majority and a referendum with a certain approval threshold.[6] This procedure was designed to last only until the end of the Althingi's following term, i.e. until 30 April 2017. The idea was to finalise the wholescale constitutional reform soon after the election instead of having to wait another four years.[7]

This temporary provision needed to be approved again by the new parliament following the election in spring 2013 in order to enter into force. The results of the general election of 27 April 2013 meant, however, that there was a diminishing prospect of having the 2011 Proposal of the Constitutional Council adopted as a new constitution. The winners of the election, i.e. the Independence Party and the Progressive Party, previously in opposition, formed a coalition, and they were sceptical of the need for a new constitution. The coalition agreement of 23 May 2013 nevertheless acknowledged the issue of the constitutional revision, therefore signalling a willingness to make progress in cooperation with the other political parties.[8] The new parliament did confirm the temporary constitutional revision procedure adopted before the election as Constitutional Act 91/2013.[9] At the same time the political parties in parliament agreed to establish a new Constitutional Committee,[10] which was appointed by the Prime Minister.[11] The Committee had nine members; the two coalition parties nominated two members each, and the four opposition parties nominated one member each. The chairperson was appointed by Prime Minister Sigmunður David Gunnlaugsson (Progressive Party), without nomination.[12] The first chairman of the Committee was Sigurður Líndal, Emeritus

6 The essence of the temporary reform procedure under Constitutional Act 91/2013 was as follows. If Parliament approves a constitutional bill with at least two-thirds of the votes cast, it shall be submitted to a binding referendum. The referendum shall take place no sooner than six months after the parliamentary approval and no later than nine months. In order to pass, the bill needs to be approved by the majority of valid votes which is not less than 40% of all registered voters. Subsequently it shall be confirmed by the President of the Republic and become a valid constitutional law.

7 According to Article 79 of the Constitution, amendments can only be adopted in connection with parliamentary elections.

8 'The revision of the Constitution of the Republic will continue aiming for broad agreement and professionalism. Emphasis will be placed on a provision on national ownership of resources and on referendums on laws from Parliament at the request of a substantial part of the electorate. In accordance with the present constitutional framework, the revision will take place under the auspices and responsibility of Althingi which will take work from previous years into account. Emphasis will be placed on transparency and informed debate with the participation of the general public.' [unofficial translation] See: www.stjornarradid.is/efst-a-baugi/frettir/stok-frett/2013/05/23/Stefnuyfirlysing-rikisstjornar-Framsoknarflokksins-og-Sjalfstaedisflokksins/

9 Article 79 continued to be valid, so for four years, there were two possible procedures to amend the Constitution.

10 See also: Chapter 13 by Katrín Jakobsdóttir, who discusses the Committee's work and its proposals.

11 Memorandum of 2 July 2013. The Pirate Party refused to sign the Memorandum, but they later agreed to join the Committee before it started its work.

12 By convention, constitutional matters fall within the remit of the Prime Minister.

Professor in law (University of Iceland).[13] However, due to health reasons, he had to relinquish his post on 1 September 2014, and the Prime Minister decided to replace him with me.[14] The Committee was faced with a difficult task as it would be hard to find a compromise which proponents of wholescale reform and those advocating a piecemeal revision could live with. Furthermore, the battles related to the constitutional project of the previous government had left many scars.

The Committee adopted a work schedule, setting out how they intended to proceed and a public consultation plan. The first task was to compose a discussion document outlining issues to be dealt with as a matter of priority. The idea was to finalise proposals on these first, so that they might be put to a binding referendum towards the middle of the term as permitted by the temporary clause of Constitutional Act 91/2013 mentioned previously. Then the Committee would look into other issues. This plan turned out to be too optimistic. During the three years of work, the Committee only managed to deal with the priority issues, and its work was interrupted by the early election of 29 October 2016 following a political crisis related to the so-called Panama Papers in the spring that year.

The Committee identified four priority issues as outlined in the 'discussion document' (*Áfangaskýrsla*) issued in June 2014.[15] They were referendums requested by the electorate, transfer of State sovereignty in the framework of international cooperation, national ownership of natural resources and environmental protection. Two of these issues, namely natural resources and direct democracy, had already featured high on the political agenda during the previous term, and they had been the object of specific questions in the 2012 advisory referendum. Transfer of State sovereignty was considered important by the Committee as the 1944 Constitution is silent on the conditions for sharing State powers with other States within international organisations. Parliament has repeatedly dealt with such questions due to Iceland's participation in the European Economic Area (EEA) but without any explicit constitutional provision on where the limits are and which process to follow.[16] The issue of environmental protection was considered to be logically connected to that of natural resources.

13 Other members of the Committe were Ms. Aðalheiður Ámundadóttir (Pirate Party), Mr. Birgir Ármannsson (Independence Party), Ms. Freyja Haraldsdóttir (Bright Future), Mr. Jón Kristjánsson (Progressive Party), Ms. Katrín Jakobsdóttir (Left-Greens), Mr. Skúli Magnússon (Progressive Party), Ms. Valgerður Bjarnadóttir (Social Democratic Party), and Ms. Valgerður Gunnarsdóttir (Independence Party). Freyja was later succeeded by Mr. Páll Valur Björnsson, then by Ms. Valgerður Björk Pálsdóttir, and finally by Róbert Marshall. Skúli was later replaced by Mr. Einar Hugi Bjarnason.

14 Since 2009, I had headed the Department of Legislative Affairs in the Prime Minister's Office. Constitutional law and its evolution are one of the tasks of that Office.

15 www.stjornarradid.is/media/forsaetisraduneyti-media/media/stjornarskra/starf-stjornarskrarnefndar-1-afangaskyrsla.pdf

16 When Iceland joined the European Economic Area in 1993, it was decided that a constitutional amendment was not needed. As time passed, the Icelandic authorities were repeatedly confronted with the question about the extent to which the Constitution allowed State powers to be transferred to international organisations. For quite some time, it has therefore been a prevalent opinion in the legal community in Iceland that a constitutional provision was needed to define the limits of this practice

Following the publication of the discussion document, the Committee started developing proposals on the four priority issues. Expert groups were appointed to assist the Committee, one for each issue.[17] Each expert group received a carefully drafted and negotiated mandate, and they delivered their proposals to the Committee in early summer 2015 in the form of draft constitutional amendments.[18] At the time, the Committee intended to have proposals ready in the form of draft constitutional bills in September 2015. The idea was that if parliament adopted the bills, a binding referendum (based on the previously mentioned temporary revision clause) could then be organised in parallel with the presidential elections due in June 2016.[19] However, President Mr. Ólafur Ragnar Grímsson heavily criticised this plan in a speech at the opening of parliament in September 2015. In particular, he warned against encroaching on the sovereignty of the Republic. He was also opposed to the idea of holding a referendum alongside the presidential elections, finding this to be 'undemocratic.'[20] In October, he elaborated further in a radio

---

and the process for granting authorisation for it. See e.g.: Björg Thorarensen, 'Stjórnarskrárákvæði um framsal ríkisvalds – þarfar eða óþarfar breytingar á stjórnarskrá?' [Constitutional Provisions on Transfer of Sovereign Powers – Useful or Unnecessary Changes to the Constitution?] in *Fullveldi í 99 ár, safn ritgerða til heiðurs dr. Davíð Þór Björgvinssyni sextugum* [Sovereignty for 99 Years – A Collection of Essays Honouring Dr. Davíð Thor Björgvinsson] (The Icelandic Literary Society 2017) 113–142.

17 The Constitutional Committee agreed on the composition of the expert committees and their mandate. The Prime Minister's Office negotiated a contract with each of them. The experts included the following: on natural resources: Supreme Court Judge Mr. Karl Axelsson, District Court Judge Mr. Skúli Magnússon, Professor of Economics Mr. Daði Már Kristófersson, and Ms. Aagot Óskarsdóttir, lawyer; on environmental protection: Ms. Ellý Katrín Guðmundsdóttir, lawyer, and Associate Professor and political assistant to the Minister of the Interior Ms. Kristín Haraldsdóttir; on transfer of State powers: Professor Ms. Björg Thorarensen, Ambassador Mr. Kristján Andri Stefánsson, and University Lecturer Mr. Arnaldur Hjartarson; on referendums: Professor of Political Science Mr. Ólafur Þ. Harðarson, Professor of Law Ms. Ragnhildur Helgadóttir, and Ms. Dóra Guðmundsdóttir, lawyer.

18 The experts' proposals were not published, and in general the work of the experts was rather low profile. Everybody involved understood that such proposals were of limited value and interest if not supported by the Committee. In fact, the Committee made some further changes to the proposals before making them public, and the proposals regarding the transfer of sovereignty were never published at all.

19 The Committee's plan was outlined in an interview with its chairman in *Morgunblaðið* [Icelandic daily newspaper, traditionally close to the Independence Party] on 31 August 2015. In retrospect, this interview may have been premature since at that time the Prime Minister and other Cabinet Ministers reserved their position on questions relating to the constitutional revision.

20 After having outlined the importance of sovereignty for Icelanders, the President remarked: 'At present, however, it is announced in the name of a Committee, which discusses the Constitution, that the new Parliament must in the next few weeks change this cornerstone of the Icelandic Constitution; they claim that time is short and that, for reasons of saving money and efficiency, the presidential elections next spring should be used [for the referendum as well]. The material reasons are not a reference to national wellbeing nor broad public support, but rather some general talk about international cooperation, legal technicalities and the wishes of bureaucrats. Iceland has, since the Republic was founded, succeeded in conducting various international relations within the UN, Nordic Council, NATO, EFTA and other organisations [. . .] without a need to change the sovereignty clauses of the Republic; the holy heritage of independence.' (author's translation), at http://wayback.vefsafn.is/wayback/20150915163600/www.forseti.is/media/PDF/2015_09_08_Thingsetning_2015.pdf

interview and criticised the political horse-trading related to the Constitution going on between the political parties.[21] Some of this criticism certainly included valid arguments, but the President did not directly address the main reasons for the Committee's particular time frame. Namely, that it was considered important to use the temporary provision under Constitutional Act 91/2013 to ensure a continuity with the work on the constitutional reform during the Althingi's previous term. That provision required that the majority in favour reflected at least 40% of registered voters. Hence it was obvious that sufficient participation might be a problem if the referendum and the presidential election were to be organised separately.

This intervention by the President slowed down the process,[22] and the Constitutional Committee did not finalise its proposals until February 2016. Furthermore, serious reservations arose regarding the sovereignty question, not in the Committee itself but rather within the two coalition parties, and so the Committee had to give up making a proposal on this issue.[23] As a result, the Committee published only three draft bills for consultation on 19 February 2016.

The three draft bills were made available for public consultation for two weeks and a considerable number of comments were sent in.[24] The Committee went through the comments, and some minor changes were made to the documents.[25] On 1 July 2016, the Committee delivered its draft bills to the Prime Minister. Attached were separate opinions by all members of the Committee emphasising particular points and, in some cases, regretting that some comments received during the public consultation had not been taken appropriately into account.[26] Nevertheless, it can be maintained that the draft bills reflected a compromise within the Committee

21 Interview in the Sunday Morning Radio Programme *Sprengisandur* [the name refers to a large highland desert in the middle of Iceland] at Bylgjan Radio Station on 11 October 2015.

22 The President's popularity and standing had grown considerably after he refused to sign two bills related to the so-called Icesave issue, leading to referendums in 2010 and 2011, as a result of which the deals with the UK and the Netherlands related to debts of Icelandic banks were rejected.

23 The Independence Party (*Sjálfstæðisflokkurinn*) held its biannual congress in October 2015, and the final resolution made no mention of the transfer of state powers issue; see: https://xd.is/wp-content/uploads/2016/09/Stjornskipunar-og-eftirlitsnefnd-Landsfundur-Sjalfstaedisflokksins-2015.pdf. This demonstrated a lack of support within the party for such a provision at that time. Committee members representing the Progressive party (*Framsóknarflokkurinn*) also reported that concerns had been raised about the same issue when they presented the status of the work to the parliamentary group of their party.

24 The comments are available on the official website dedicated to constitutional reform: www.stjornarradid.is/verkefni/stjornskipan-og-thjodartakn/stjornarskrain/stjornarskrarnefnd-2013-2017/samrad/

25 As the public discussion on the Committee proposals progressed, serious misgivings were raised both within the Social Democratic Party (*Samfylkingin*) and the Pirate Party (*Píratar*), i.e. within the two parties that were most supportive of the 2011 Constitutional Council's Proposal. For the former, it was mainly the wording of the provision on national resources and the Explanatory Notes that were criticised, and for the latter it was mainly the provision on direct democracy which was considered too restrictive.

26 www.stjornarradid.is/media/forsaetisraduneyti-media/media/stjornarskra/bokanir-allar.pdf

as regards their broad lines. Formally, the Committee proposed three separate draft bills, each containing a new article to be added at the end of the 1944 Constitution, namely Articles 79, 80, and 81, with the current Article 79 (on constitutional revision) intended to become Article 82. When they were introduced in parliament by the Prime Minister, they were merged into one constitutional bill (*frumvarp til stjórnarskipunarlaga*), without any change being made to their content.[27] The text referred to here is that of the constitutional bill as introduced to parliament by interim Prime Minister Sigurður Ingi Jóhannsson (Progressive Party).

Although the Committee delivered draft constitutional bills regarding three of the four priority issues that they identified at the start of their work, there was no sense of triumph amongst its members when it disbanded in July 2016. Time had run out. An early parliamentary election was looming, following the Panama Papers scandal in the spring 2016. Within some of the opposition parties, there were misgivings about the outcome of the Committee's work, and their representatives on the Committee did not have the conviction or the standing in their parties to gather the necessary support. It also needs to be borne in mind that the two coalition parties were anyway reluctant supporters of the proposals. Therefore, when Prime Minister Sigurður Ingi Jóhannsson introduced the proposals in the form of a constitutional bill in parliament on 25 August 2016, it was more for the record than in the belief that they would be passed before the general election, which then took place on 29 October 2016.[28] Let us look more closely at each of the three proposals of the Committee.

Protection of the environment: proposed new Article 79 of the 1944 Constitution

The constitutional bill of August 2016 reads as follows:[29]

> Iceland's nature is the foundation of all life in the land. Responsibility for protecting nature and the environment is shared collectively by all and the protection shall be based on precaution and long-term vision guided by sustainable development. The maintenance of natural diversity shall be promoted and the productivity and prosperity of ecosystems.
>
> Everyone shall enjoy a healthy environment. The public may roam freely and stay on the land for legitimate purposes. Nature shall be well treated and

27 The Explanatory Notes (greinargerðir) to the bills are quite extensive, as is the usual practice in Iceland regarding both constitutional bills and legislative bills. As chairman of the Committee, I was responsible for the drafting, but I relied on advice from some of the same experts as made the original proposals. The Explanatory Notes were then submitted to the Committee for approval.

28 Parliamentary Document 1577–841 case: www.althingi.is/altext/145/s/1577.html. The bill was presented in first reading. The relevant Parliamentary Committee sent it out for public consultation and received input from nine individuals and legal entities. No report was adopted by the Committee on the bill, and it never went to second reading.

29 This is discussed in more detail in Chapter 11 by Aðalheiður Jóhannsdóttir in this collection.

> the interests of landowners and other right holders respected. More detailed provisions for the content and extent of the right to roam shall be made by law.
>
> The right of the public to access information on the environment and the effects of any developments thereon and to participate in the preparation of decisions affecting the environment, shall be provided for by law.

This proposal was the result of analysis of constitutional provisions in other countries,[30] together with previous proposals in Iceland, starting with the proposal of the 1983 Constitutional Committee[31] and including the 2011 Constitutional Council's Proposal for a New Constitution. What proved to be most difficult was the wording of the right to roam (*almannaréttur*) in the second paragraph. While some Committee members wanted this right to be as unrestrained as possible, others emphasised the right of landowners to limit access to their land. The solution consisted of deferring this question to future legislation.[32]

Furthermore, some Committee members would have liked to see a special reference to the protection of unspoiled wilderness. They were also disappointed that the proposal incorporated only two pillars from the Aarhus Convention, namely access to information and the right to participate in decisions, but not the third on access to justice.[33]

Public ownership of natural resources: proposed Article 80 of the 1944 Constitution[34]

The constitutional bill of August 2016 reads as follows:

> Iceland's natural resources belong to the Icelandic people. They shall be utilised sustainably and for the benefit of all inhabitants. The State controls and oversees the management and utilisation of these resources on behalf of the people.
>
> Natural resources and territories that are not subject to private property rights fall under national ownership [*þjóðareign*]. Nobody can obtain ownership or permanent utilisation in respect of these resources and territories and rights pertaining to them. These resources and territories may never be sold or pledged. The legislature and the executive hold the right to their control and disposal on behalf of the people.

30 Provisions in the constitutions of Norway, Sweden, and Finland were analysed.
31 Document 537 at the 105th legislative period 1982–1983.
32 The Explanatory Notes to the constitutional bill with the three proposals of the Constitutional Committee read: 'Thus, it would be the task of the legislator to assess whether there is a need to have special provisions in law on the organisation, control and special protection mechanisms because of increased strain on nature caused by a large number of tourists.'
33 www.stjornarradid.is/media/forsaetisraduneyti-media/media/stjornarskra/bokanir-allar.pdf
34 See also: Chapter 10 by Ragnheiður Elfa Þorsteinsdóttir in this collection.

> As a general rule, an appropriate fee [*eðlilegt gjald*] shall be charged for authorisations to utilise natural resources and territories belonging to the Icelandic State or those falling under national ownership. The granting of usage authorisations shall be based on law and equality and transparency shall be respected. Such authorisations never lead to permanent ownership or irrevocable control over natural resources or territories that fall under national ownership [*þjóðareign*].

When developing this provision, the Committee built on an extensive discussion about the need for a constitutional provision on natural resources which goes back to the year 1983.[35] Little inspiration could be sought from abroad.[36] The prominence of this issue in the public discussion can only be understood in the context of profound changes in the fisheries regime over the past decades. A system of transferable quotas was introduced in the 1980s, increasing the efficiency and sustainability of fishing, while at the same time creating fewer and bigger companies that possess most of the fishing rights. This system was introduced without significant fees being paid by the fishing companies to the State. This left many Icelanders with the impression that marine resources had been privatised with a handful of persons benefitting enormously.[37]

Although any provision on the topic will have to deal with natural resources in general, the public discussion tends to focus on fishing resources. Many expect such a provision to somehow overturn the current system of transferable quotas, which they consider unjust. Others would at least like to try and stop any further 'privatisation' of common resources, and in particular prevent other resources from being subjected to the same fate. A third group of people is mainly interested in maintaining the status quo and in making sure that the constitutional provision is as neutral as possible. The 2016 proposal extends beyond fishing resources and covers in principle *all* natural resources, i.e. including mineral resources, biological, water, air, sunlight, etc. Moreover, it is not of importance whether the natural resources can be harnessed for financial gain. Rather, what is emphasised is that all utilisation shall be sustainable and for the benefit of every Icelander.

35 Former Prime Minister and Law Professor, Gunnar Thoroddsen, proposed such a constitutional provision already in 1983. His proposal stated that the natural resources of the country should be an inalienable ownership of Icelanders: document 537 at the 105th legislative period 1982–1983. This wording took inspiration from a law from 1928 on the national park of Thingvellir.

36 Only few Western democracies have a provision on natural resources in their Constitution. Furthermore, where such provisions exist, they do not enter into the detail which had become the point of reference in the Icelandic discussion, notably following the work of the Constitutional Council.

37 A description of the system is found in the UN Human Rights Committee, communication no. 1306/2004 (of 24 October 2007), CCPR/C/87/D/1306/2004. The communication concluded that the system was in violation of Article 26 of the UN Covenant: 'While not required to address the compatibility of quota systems for the use of limited resources with the Covenant as such, the Committee concludes that, in the particular circumstances of the present case, the property entitlement privilege accorded permanently to the original quota owners, to the detriment of the authors [of the complaint], is not based on reasonable grounds.'

Another crucial issue was that of property rights, and the Committee agreed early on to use the term 'national ownership' (*þjóðareign*) which had from time to time been criticised for being void of meaning. This concession by those in the Committee who favoured a more traditional approach to what ownership means was certainly necessary in order to break the path for any agreement on the matter. 'National ownership' only applies to certain natural resources, namely to those which are not already subject to private ownership, and this concept differs from 'belonging to the people' (*tilheyri þjóðinni*), which is a term used to denote another kind of relationship between natural resources and the people.[38] The proposal subjects all natural resources which do not fall under traditional ownership (whether owned by the State, or by local authorities or private parties) to 'national ownership.' This would mean that they could not be sold and any licence to utilise them should only be temporary or revocable.[39] The most difficult task of the Committee on this issue was how to formulate the provision on the rent to be paid for utilisation of national property. This difficulty goes back to the work of the Constitutional Council and its 2011 Proposal, which used the term 'full price' (*fullt verð*) under Article 34 on natural resources, according to which the 'full price' should be collected without exception. Critics of that approach maintained that the State should have a leeway to decide how to determine the rent, not necessarily auctioning off utilisation rights to obtain the highest possible price. Furthermore, the Committee decided that, in some cases, the State should be able to decide not to charge for utilisation of natural resources in national ownership, e.g. for the sake of research. The Committee found a compromise, stipulating that in principle, an 'appropriate fee' (*eðlilegt gjald*) should be charged, meaning that there might be exceptions.

When the proposal was made public in February 2016, as the Committee's chairman, I explained to the media that, if adopted, it would not as such bring about changes to the current fishing regime but that it went as far as possible to allow any future majority in Parliament to make changes. Apparently in some circles this statement was interpreted as demonstrating the proposal's uselessness.[40]

38 The Explanatory Notes to the constitutional bill of the Constitutional Committee read: 'This wording does not refer to traditional property rights but rather to the idea that Iceland's natural resources are a good which the whole nation has great interests in and in that sense, it is a common good. In this sense natural resources belong to the people irrespective of whether they are subject to private ownership, State ownership or the ownership of local authorities or that they are in national ownership.'

39 Currently, sectoral laws on different types of natural resources do not necessarily state whether they can be sold or not. For example, there is no prohibition on sale in the law on public land (*þjóðlendulög*), law on the seabed, law on fossil fuels, or the law on fisheries management. However, the law on fisheries management stipulates that the granting of utilisation rights under the law does not lead to ownership or irrevocable rights. Laws on water rights (used for hydropower plants or geothermal plants), however, stipulate since 2008 that any utilisation rights over water resources in public ownership can be granted for a maximum only 65 years. Furthermore, according to laws in this field, it is prohibited for public entities to sell, directly or indirectly, water utilisation rights to private parties.

40 Within the Pirate Party and the Social Democratic Party, the Explanatory Notes were also criticised for being too status quo oriented.

Abrogative referendum: proposed Article 81 of the 1944 Constitution

The 1944 Constitution envisages a referendum in three different cases. Firstly, under Article 11, when the President is removed from office, Parliament initiates the process (with a three-quarter majority), and the people decide in a referendum. Secondly, under Article 26, the President can refuse to confirm a law adopted by Parliament. In that case, the statute nevertheless enters into effect, but a referendum has to be organised as soon as possible to decide on its future validity. Thirdly, under Article 79 paragraph 2, when the Parliament decides to change the provision in Article 62 on the evangelical Lutheran Church being the national Church in Iceland, the statute must then be submitted to a referendum for a final decision.

The 1944 Constitution was adopted in a referendum held on 20–23 May 1944. Since then, the only constitutionally mandated referendums took place in 2010 and 2011 when the President refused to confirm bills relating to the settlement of the Icesave dispute with the UK and the Netherlands.[41] In 2004, the President had also refused to confirm a law on media concentration, but parliament avoided a referendum in that case by abolishing the adopted bill in question.

It is fair to say that when the President used his prerogative under Article 26 of the Constitution for the first time in 2004, the question of whether to increase possibilities for direct democracy came into focus and attracted significant public interest. The Constitutional Committee that operated from 2005–2007 concluded that such possibilities should be augmented; however, there was no agreement on how to do this, nor on what would be the role of the President under a new regime in this field.[42] In 2011, the Constitutional Council proposed far-reaching innovations in this respect. According to Article 65 of the Council's Proposal, 10% of the electorate could request a binding referendum on newly confirmed bills. Furthermore, according to Article 66 of that Proposal, 2% of the electorate could submit a 'bill' to the Parliament. If 10% of the electorate support this bill and if it is not adopted by Parliament, a referendum would have to take place. This would be so unless proponents of the bill decided to withdraw it, for example because a compromise bill is put forward by Parliament. In these situations, Parliament could decide beforehand that the referendum is binding. The proposal of August 2016 reads as follows:

> Fifteen per cent of eligible voters can demand that a newly confirmed law from Althingi be put to a general, secret and binding vote. The demand shall be submitted to the Minister within six weeks from the publication of the law

41 The Icesave dispute was finally settled with a judgment of the EFTA Court in case E-16/11, *EFTA Surveillance Authority v. Iceland*, delivered on 28 January 2013. For further discussion in this collection see Chapter 3 by Ágúst Þór Árnason and Catherine Dupré and Chapter 4 by Kristrún Heimisdóttir.

42 Endurskoðun stjórnarskrárinnar: Áfangaskýrsla nefndar um endurskoðun stjórnarskrár lýðveldisins Íslands, febrúar 2007, þskj. 1293–709. mál., einkum bls. 8–13 [Revision of the Constitution: Interim Report of the Committee to Revise the Constitution of the Republic of Iceland, February 2007, document 1293, case 709, 133rd legislative period]; see in particular pp. 8–13.

> and the vote shall take place no earlier than six weeks and no later than four months after a certified demand has been submitted. The budget, supplementary budgets, acts on matters concerning taxation and laws adopted to fulfil obligations under international law will not be put to a referendum according to this paragraph.
>
> Fifteen per cent of eligible voters can furthermore demand that a resolution by Althingi according to article 21 [ratification of treaties] be put to a general, secret and binding vote. A law that is adopted by two-thirds of votes in Althingi may stipulate that the same applies to resolutions that have legal implications or contain important policy formulations. The demand must be received by the Minister within six weeks from the adoption by Althingi and the vote shall take place no earlier than six weeks and no later than four months after a certified demand has been submitted.
>
> Althingi may rescind a law or repeal a resolution before a referendum takes place, in which case it will not be held.
>
> To reject a law or resolution according to this article, a majority in a referendum, but no less than a quarter of eligible voters, must vote against it.
>
> A law adopted by two-thirds of votes in Althingi shall further provide for start dates and representation for petitions, the form and collection of signatures, the dissemination of information, the implementation of referendums and settlement of disputes in court.

Article 80 on direct democracy is probably the most original of the Committee's three proposals. Less groundwork had been done on this question in the past than in relation to the other two issues. One of the reasons is certainly that the President had not used his veto powers at all until 2004, and then only again in 2010 and 2011 in relation to the Icesave issue. This had triggered the pressing question as to whether one person, namely the President, should be the only one able to provoke a binding referendum on statutes adopted by the Parliament. As discussed previously, in 2011 the Constitutional Council dealt with the matter and proposed far-reaching provisions introducing new direct democracy instruments.

The Constitutional Committee agreed at the outset that it would only propose a provision regarding the right of voters to initiate a referendum on newly adopted statutes, and that it would not formulate a provision containing the right to initiate new law. Furthermore, it decided not to follow the Danish model of giving the minority in Parliament the right to initiate a referendum on statutes.[43] Some members of the Committee favoured such an approach, but they were not in a majority. The Committee studied provisions in other countries and found that very few 'old' democracies in Europe have such constitutionally protected means of direct

43 According to Article 42 of the Danish Constitution, one-third of the members of Parliament can request a referendum on newly adopted laws. For the law to be abrogated, a majority of those taking part in the referendum must vote against, and this majority has to represent at least 30% of all voters.

democracy, i.e. only Switzerland, Liechtenstein, and Italy, with the Danish solution being somewhat different. This comparative exercise helped the Committee conclude that it would be wise to tread cautiously in this field. The example of Slovenia, where a very progressive constitution had been adopted and later amended to narrow down direct democracy elements, was instructive in this respect.[44]

The proposal of the Committee represents a compromise solution as all the parties had different opinions. The Pirates Party, in particular, was in favour of no or low thresholds, and the Independence Party advocated moderate or considerable thresholds. In my view as the Committee's chairman, it is remarkable that the parties were at all able to agree on a proposal that nobody could even have imagined ten years earlier. The work of the Constitutional Council in 2011 certainly laid the groundwork for this to be possible. The proposal of the Committee contains several important features:

- Fifteen per cent of the electorate could request a binding referendum on newly confirmed statutes and other important decisions. Here, a compromise was found between the 10% proposed by the Constitutional Council and the 20% or more suggested by some of the members of the Committee.
- The right to initiate a referendum would be applied not only to statutes but also to parliamentary resolutions in relation to the ratification of international treaties, according to Article 21 of the 1944 Constitution.[45] Those resolutions are necessary to enable the ratification of international treaties when they require amendments to Icelandic law. In this way, the proposal grants the possibility to subject the most important international treaties to referendums.[46] Furthermore, the proposal authorises Parliament to adopt a law by a majority of two-thirds, enhancing further the material scope of referendums. Such a law could include resolutions with legal consequences or resolutions which contain important policy. Here, the Explanatory Notes give inter alia the example of parliamentary resolutions in the environmental field which rank hydroelectric projects according to their impact on the environment. Such a constitutional provision, if implemented by a law with qualified majority, would enable voters to block new controversial hydroelectric projects.

44 See: www.sloveniatimes.com/parliament-tightens-referendum-rules-with-constitutional-amendment

45 Article 21 of the Constitution reads: 'The President of the Republic concludes treaties with other states. Unless approved by Althingi, he may not make such treaties if they entail renouncement of, or servitude on, territory or territorial waters, or if they require changes in the State's governance.' In practice, Althingi's approval for any international treaty which calls for a change in Icelandic law is given in the form of a resolution.

46 The proposal covers the ratification of international treaties which require amendments to Icelandic law. Article 21 has never been considered a basis for transfer of sovereign powers. Iceland's participation in the European Economic Area sometimes requires transfer of sovereign powers to the EFTA Surveillance Authority or even EU bodies. In such cases, legal doctrine has struggled to find a basis in unwritten constitutional law. Any future accession to the EU would require constitutional amendments.

- There were some exceptions to the right to initiate a referendum according to the proposal. The annual budget was excluded, as well as tax laws and laws implementing international obligations. These exceptions are common in other countries with direct democracy instruments.[47] No contradiction is involved in exempting the implementation of international obligations, but at the same time allowing referendums on parliamentary resolutions in relation to new international obligations (cf. the preceding point 2). The idea is that the voters should be allowed to intervene at the right moment, i.e. before an international obligation is entered into. Once the international obligation is in place (following a resolution or exceptionally with a special statute, which could according to the proposal be put as such to a referendum), no referendum is allowed. The coherence of Iceland's position vis-à-vis the international community is thus safeguarded.
- Parliament could, at its own initiative, withdraw adopted bills or resolutions if a referendum has been requested. This can be relevant if the majority in Parliament realises that the referendum might be in favour of annulment.
- To overcome a statute or a resolution, a majority of voters would have to vote against it. In addition, this majority would have to represent at least a quarter of the electorate. This aspect of the Committee's proposal was perhaps the most controversial. Some members of the Committee were against any such thresholds, while others were in favour of even more stringent conditions. The outcome seems to represent a sensible compromise between the two. Parliament's decisions would remain intact unless opponents are able to mobilise a considerable part of the electorate. This should contribute to a cautious use of such a novelty in the constitution. It furthermore helped to overcome reservations by those who feared that it would be relatively easy, by relying on new technologies, to collect the signatures needed to initiate a referendum.
- The provision makes it clear that additional legislation would be needed to craft the details of how the proposal should work in practice. Such a law requires a qualified majority, again minimising the risk that a narrow majority in Parliament could somehow disrespect the spirit of the constitutional provision.

The proposal leaves intact the prerogative of the President to call a referendum on laws adopted by Parliament according to Article 26 of the 1944 Constitution. This may sound surprising, as one might ask why such a provision would still be needed and if it would not be contradictory to have two separate constitutional paths for challenging new statutes. Furthermore, the paths would have different characteristics, namely no material exceptions to the power of the President and no rejection threshold in the ensuing referendum. The Explanatory Notes address this issue by stating that the importance of this presidential prerogative had recently gained increased weight in the constitutional framework of the country. Although this was not explicitly stated, it

47 See e.g.: Paragraph 6 of Article 42 of the Danish Constitution and Article 90 of the Slovenian Constitution.

might be added that it did not seem politically feasible at that time to alter Article 26. It is also mentioned that there might be cases where laws merited a referendum although they fell under one of the exceptions contained in the Committee's proposal. In such cases, the President might decide to intervene. The President might also decide to use his or her power when it would make sense to carry out a referendum with some expediency. Finally, the Explanatory Notes make the point that it seemed logical to review Article 26 alongside other provisions relating to the President. It may become a pressing question whether the signature of the President should be needed for new laws. Alternatively, the President could be given a new role, e.g. referring bills adopted by Parliament to the Supreme Court for constitutional scrutiny.

Conclusion

The reader may wonder why it took three years, from May 2013 to July 2016, to conclude the work of the Committee with the modest result discussed in this chapter. Compared to the Constitutional Council, which drafted a full proposal for a new constitution within a time frame of four months, the question is justified. However, it is not necessarily fair to compare the work of a group of 25 citizens, which were given a limited time to come up with proposals, with the work of a Committee including representatives of all political parties. In the former case, the Council's members, having been originally elected, were appointed on an individual basis free from any outside mandate and from having to seek external approval for their positions. In the latter case, every sentence had to be submitted to the different political parties for preliminary approval, and the parties in many cases felt they had to defend a particular point of view, a particular political philosophy, or a particular historical approach to constitutional work and the themes on the table.

With hindsight, it is difficult to see how any other method might have succeeded, given the fact that the 2011 Proposal of the Constitutional Council failed as Parliament did not even pass a vote on it, let alone adopt it. Therefore, it is submitted that although the result of the Constitutional Committee's work was apparently modest, it nevertheless reflected a political agreement on very important matters. At the time of writing, the Constitutional revision process is being restarted under a new coalition government led by Prime Minister Katrín Jakobsdóttir from the Left-Green Movement. The issues discussed by the Constitutional Committee are, according to the published plan of the Prime Minister,[48] dealt with during the present term (2017–2021), together with other issues that the Committee did not consider. It is encouraging to see that more attention has been paid to the project design than ever before. In a vacuum, it is not overly complicated to draft new or revised constitutional provisions that make sense. The difficulty lies in forging a consensus among political parties and in society as a whole. Here, good project management and political leadership are necessary preconditions for success.

48 www.stjornarradid.is/lisalib/getfile.aspx?itemid=e6329b3c-1a68-11e9-942f-005056bc4d74

10 Natural resources and the reform of the Icelandic Constitution

Ragnheiður Elfa Þorsteinsdóttir[1]

Introduction

As is often the case with island nations, natural resources are of prime economic significance for Iceland, particularly with regard to fisheries, renewable energy, water, and land,[2] which are an important foundation of the Icelandic economy. Ownership, utilisation, and management of these resources are therefore among the most demanding and complex tasks of government, both politically and legally, and have been so for several decades. The 1944 Constitution is silent on natural resources, and in the aftermath of the 2008 financial crisis, the call for a constitutional provision on natural resources came to the center of political discussion on constitutional reform. The question of ownership of natural resources has dominated debates without leading to any general consensus on the formulation of such a provision. In a number of proposals put forward regarding a constitutional provision on natural resources a uniform approach is sought in accommodating ownership, management and utilisation, and benefit sharing.

Although traditionally ownership of natural resources has been the prevailing approach to a constitutional provision on natural resources, the development of international standards and rules has also been influential. Since the beginning of the 1990s, the concept of sustainable development has gradually

1 I would like to give my special thanks to Rachael Lorna Johnstone, Catherine Dupré, and Ágúst Þór Árnason for comments and useful discussions when working on this chapter.

2 Understanding what 'natural resources' encompass is complex, and various attempts have been made to define them, with the first definition being provided by the 2000 Opinion of the Natural Resources Committee. Since then, there has been ongoing work to describe natural resources in line with how the definition has evolved. In 2017, the minister for the environment and natural resources defined natural resources as 'being a source of input/goods in nature that can be of use for human beings (such as timber, energy, fish, air etc.)'. The idea was to classify natural resources into six main categories: (a) land, (b) sea, (c) coast, (d) water, (e) energy, and (f) wild animals in line with the UK Natural Capital Committee; see: www.althingi.is/altext/146/s/0666.html. In September 2018, the opposition called for establishing a clear *legal* definition of natural resources; see: www.althingi.is/thingstorf/thingmalalistar-eftir-thingum/ferill/?ltg=149&mnr=55. See also: Report by the committee on policy-making on natural resources established by the government in 2012, 'auðlindastefnunefnd', p. 11 at www.stjornarradid.is/media/forsaetisraduneyti-media/media/skyrslur/stefnumorkun-i-audlindamalum.pdf (all webpages last accessed 2 June 2020).

gained acceptance in Icelandic legislation as a general principle in relation to the management of natural resources. The principle of sustainable development and its dimensions,[3] which have been at the core of international cooperation initially in relation to the environment, do not though have a constitutional basis.

When discussing the need to include a provision on natural resources in the Icelandic Constitution, it is important to analyse what the aim and implications of such a provision would be.[4] Management and utilisation of natural resources have traditionally been high on the political agenda, in particular in relation to fisheries and power generation. Historically, the marine sector has been a key driver in the economy and is one of the main pillars of export activity in Iceland although it has been declining as a share of total exports since the early 1990s. In 2017, 38% of goods exports and roughly 16% of all export earnings from goods and services came from fish.[5] In economic terms, the abundance of water power and geothermal energy in the natural environment is also an important pillar of export trade.[6] Exploitation of natural resources as well as overexploitation, such as in the case of fish stocks, have had direct effect on the economy and standard of living.[7] In addition, following the financial crisis in 2008, the sharp devaluation of the currency, together with the uniqueness of Iceland's natural environment and wilderness,[8] have led to unprecedented growth in tourism and related services, which have also influenced public opinion on the importance of nature conservation. Now tourism has established itself as the third main pillar of the Icelandic economy.[9]

3 Rachel Emas, 'The Concept of Sustainable Development: Definition and Defining Principles', brief for GSDR 2015, at. https://sustainabledevelopment.un.org/content/documents/5839GSDR%20 2015_SD_concept_definiton_rev.pdf. See also: United Nations General Assembly, *Report of the World Commission on Environment and Development: Our Common Future*. Oslo, Norway: United Nations General Assembly, Development and International Co-operation: Environment, 1987.

4 'Economy of Iceland' (The Central Bank of Iceland October 2018): www.cb.is/library/Skraarsafn-EN/Economy-of-Iceland/2018/EOI_2018_heildarskjal.pdf

5 Ibid. 14, 15, and 17.

6 'Iceland Highlights,' Environmental Performance Reviews (OECD 2014): www.oecd.org/environment/country-reviews/Iceland%20Highlights%20web6.pdf

7 'Hvers virði er atvinnulíf', Iceland Chamber of Commerce, 2012 at http://vi.is/files/2012.03.12-Hvers-virdi-er-atvinnulif-net_1657613606.pdf

8 Almost half of its total area is uninhabited highland that has been described as the largest remaining wilderness in Europe: 'Economy of Iceland' (Central Bank of Iceland October 2018). See also: Þóra Ellen Þórhallsdóttir, 'Environment and Energy in Iceland: A Comparative Analysis of Values and Impacts' (2016) 27 *Environmental Impact Assessment Review* 522–544.

9 The growing interest in the wilderness and the uniqueness of the landscape, together with a sharp decrease of the currency value (Icelandic Króna) in 2008, led to unprecedented growth in tourism-related services. 'Economy of Iceland' (Central Bank of Iceland, October 2018) 19. The number of foreign tourists grew, for instance, from 470,000 in 2008 to 2.3 million in 2018: www.cb.is/library/Skraarsafn-EN/Economy-of-Iceland/2018/EOI_2018_heildarskjal.pdf. See also: 'The Icelandic Master Plan for Nature Protection and Energy Utilization.' at www.ramma.is/english

Recently concerns have been growing over land becoming subject to foreign ownership in spite of the legal restrictions already in place against the acquisition of land by foreigners.[10] Ownership and control over land give control over natural resources that again encompasses economic and political power. These restrictions, however, include important exemptions mainly under the European Economic Area (EEA) Agreement for those who enjoy rights under the four freedoms.

In this context, a number of proposals for a new constitutional provision on natural resources have been introduced over recent decades, both by the Althingi and by non-parliamentary specialist committees established for that purpose, with the first one coming from a member of the opposition in the parliament in 1963. This chapter considers the main legislative provisions on natural resources and discusses proposals that were put forward for a constitutional provision on natural resources. Particular attention is given to the 2011 Proposal for a New Constitution and the 2012 Constitutional Bill, as well as to Article 80 of the 2016 Constitutional Bill. The strong public interest behind the necessity to codify a constitutional provision on natural resources has been highly influential on how proposals for constitutional provisions have developed over time. Since the publication of the Natural Resources Committee Opinion in 2000,[11] the constitutional reform discussion on natural resources has involved three main issues, firstly and above all the question of ownership, secondly the question of definition, and thirdly the question of use, namely benefit-sharing and the requirement of sustainability, as evidenced, for instance, in the 2016 Constitutional Bill. All of these issues are and will be politically sensitive. The chapter seeks to contribute to the discussion by suggesting a shift in focus from the mainstream issue of ownership to that of how best to use natural resources for the benefit of all, that is, a focus on administrative implementation, management, and conditions for resource use.[12]

10 'The conditions for entitlement to own and use real estate in Iceland are set in the Act 19/1966 on the Right of Ownership and Use of Real Property. These rights also include fishing and hunting rights, water rights, and other real property rights, whether acquired by free assignation or enforcement measures, marriage, inheritance, or transfer of deed. The general principle under the Act is that Icelandic nationals and foreign nationals domiciled in Iceland may own property in the country or acquire the rights to its use. Legal entities must satisfy certain requirements to own real estate in Iceland.', Ministry of Justice: www.government.is/topics/foreign-nationals/foreign-nationals-real-property-rights/

11 'Opinion of the Natural Resources Committee' (2000): www.stjornarradid.is/media/forsaetisraduneyti-media/media/Skyrslur/Skyrsla_Audlindanefndar_final.pdf

12 Leo-Felix Lee, 'Sovereignty over, Ownership of, and Access to Natural Resources' in Dan Tarlock and John C. Dernbach (eds), *Environmental Laws and Their Enforcement* – Vol. II. A. (EOLSS Publications 2009) 3: 'Ownership coordinates the conduct among individuals, whereas sovereignty coordinates the conduct among independent states.' Also: 'Private property in natural resources has always existed in the legal systems of the world. Correspondingly, such property has ever since been restricted to the benefit of the public,' 2.

No constitutional provision on natural resources, but a rich body of statutes

Natural resources law

Natural resources law covers not only property rights or ownership rights but also rules on management, use, and protection of natural resources. The first of these is a matter of private property law, whereas the last refers to the administrative aspect of natural resources, such as environmental protection and nature conservation, that has been described as being much more important today.[13]

Legislation on the administration and management of natural resources has proliferated, not least because of Iceland's membership of the EEA, in which the parties to the Agreement undertook inter alia to ensure a prudent and rational utilisation of natural resources based, in particular, on the principle of sustainable development.[14] Examples include water and energy use but do not, however, affect property rights over natural resources.[15]

Icelandic legislation on natural resources can be described as falling mainly under four categories: fisheries, water, ground resources, and nature conservation. Such provisions have different approaches and do not necessarily have a harmonised aim of conservation based on sustainable development and utilisation. Most often, such provisions provide for both ownership and utilisation or management of natural resources, irrespective of whether they come under private ownership or private property rights.

Ownership and management of natural resources

Legislation on various natural resources has long existed in Iceland, such as that on water, both in relation to use rights and management of natural resources. Natural resources that can be subject to private ownership are to a large extent under private ownership, generally established by law and usually attached to ownership

13 'Administrative resolution of conflicting claims to a resource is vastly more important today than judicial determination of property rights.': Robert L. Fischmann, 'What Is Natural Resources Law?' (2007) *Articles by Maurer Faculty*. Paper 197, 178 (www.repository.law.indiana.edu/cgi/viewcontent.cgi?article=1197&context=facpub). Such distinction has been described as having the purpose of specifying what sources can be owned and the terms of legal rights or use rights and secondly to facilitate resource-related transactions such as licences, leases, and sales. Eric T. Freyfogle, 'Natural Resources Law' in *Berkshire Encyclopedia of Sustainability: The Law and Polititics of Sustainability* (Berkshire Publishing 2011) 396: www.berkshirepublishing.com/assets/pdf/Natural_Resources_Law_Freyfogle.pdf

14 Preamble of the EEA Agreement and Article 73, para 1 (c) of the EEA-Agreement.

15 Judgement in the Case E-2/06 – *EFTA Surveillance Authority v. Norway*, 26 June 2007: 'The Court holds that Article 125 EEA is to be interpreted to the effect that an EEA State's right to decide whether hydropower resources and related installations are in private or public ownership is, as such, not affected by the EEA Agreement.'

of land.[16] Land is divided into three main categories, namely private land, public land, and upland ranges.[17] Private land is land subject to private property rights according to law. Public land is defined as land that is not subject to private ownership and is declared by law to be owned by the Icelandic State.[18] Upland ranges (*afréttur*) is understood as an area which is outside inhabited areas and subject to use rights, including summer grazing for sheep and possibly some other use rights, but which is not usually subject to ownership, either privately or publicly, such as by municipalities or the State.[19]

The exploitable marine stocks of the Icelandic fishing banks were already declared by statute in 1988 to be common property of the Icelandic nation, with the aim of the law also being to ensure their preservation and economical (*hagkvæm nýting*) utilisation.[20] In 1996, in the Act 57/1996 on the Treatment of Commercial Marine Stocks, sustainable utilisation was introduced for the purpose of improving the treatment of commercial marine stocks and to ensure the maximum long-term return for the Icelandic nation.[21]

Ownership, management and utilisation of ground resources, such as ground water and geothermal energy, are also governed by law. The right to utilise water, in terms of both consumption and hydropower, is attached to ownership of land.[22]

16 See e.g.: Skúli Magnússon: 'Constitutional Provision on Resources', in *Report of the Constitutional Commission* (vol I) 233: www.stjornlagarad.is/other_files/stjornlagarad/skyrsla-stjornlaganefndar/skyrsla_stjornlaganefndar_fyrra_bindi.pdf. See also: pp. 225–249, pp. 230 and 233.

17 In 1998, a statute was adopted for the purpose of solving a long-standing dispute on the determination of the boundaries of private land, public land, and upland ranges. This was done by dividing all land into three main categories: private land, public land, and upland ranges; see: Act 58/1998 on Common Land and Boundaries of Private Land, Common Land and Highland Pasture (Common Land Act). The Act provides for the utilisation of natural resources such as water, wind power, and mines within public land. Such utilisation is subject to permission by the state, and fees to be paid for such utilisation.

18 Article 1 of the 1998 Common Land Act.

19 See further: frumvarp til laga um þjóðlendur og ákvörðun marka eignarlanda, þjóðlendna og afrétta, þingskjal 598–367. mál, 122. löggjafarþing 1997–1998, pp. 4–5.

20 Article 1 of Act 3/1988 on Fisheries Management 1988–1990; see also: frumvarp til laga um stjórn fiskveiða 1988–1991, þskj. 201, 181. mál, 110. löggjafarþing 1987 and Article 1 of Fisheries Management Act 116/2006 at http://extwprlegs1.fao.org/docs/texts/ice3455.doc

21 Article 1 of Act 57/1996 on the Treatment of Commercial Marine Stocks.

22 Iceland is rich in water resources, both in terms of quality and quantity. Long-term conservation, management and surveillance, access to sufficient pure water, and the rights of the landowner are to be found in two main statutes – Act 36/2011 on water governance and the Water Act 15/1923 (as amended) – that provide for integration of utilisation and environmental protection of the aquatic resources through preventive measures and sustainable development. The rights of the landowner are, however, limited in relation to the utilisation of hydropower for electricity production for profit. The construction and operation of an electric power plant is also subject to a licence issued by the National Energy Authority. As with fishing rights, the right to utilise water is attached to ownership of land and subject to statute law. The Ground Resources Act 57/1998 on the Survey and Utilization of Ground Resources addresses both ownership, management, and utilisation, see e.g.: Article 3. It includes resources in the ground, at the bottom of rivers and lakes, and at the bottom of the sea within netting limits (Article 1). The Act applies to any element, compound, and energy that can

Moreover, rights in relation to freshwater, such as fishing rights, are also as a general rule attached to land ownership.[23] In the case of seabed resources, the Icelandic State's ownership outside netting limits falls under the sovereign rights of Iceland and has been stated by law.[24]

Utilisation of natural resources owned by private parties or covered by private property rights is usually subject to public management and is restricted in some ways. Most often the aim is to ensure efficient use of resources or to protect the public interest. For instance, the Act 15/1923 on Water provides for the right of a municipality to access and use surface water on private property or water subject to private property rights. Under certain conditions, the municipality can resort to expropriation if an agreement with the land or rights owner is not possible (Article 27). Another example is research and utilisation of resources in the ground subject to a licence of the National Energy Authority, which lays down requirements and procedures for research and utilisation that are subject to Nature Conservation Act 60/2013.[25]

The last category in relation to Icelandic legislation on natural resources is nature conservation. With the Nature Conservation Act 60/2013, an enhanced integrated approach was taken to include sustainable development and natural resources in light of international obligations and the three economic, social, and environmental dimensions of sustainable development.

Finally, provisions on fees, charges, and distribution of benefits are scattered in current legislation. The system for fees or taxes for utilisation of the fisheries resources of Iceland was, for example, introduced in 2012, whereby fishing fees are imposed for the purpose of meeting the cost of state research, control, management in relation to fisheries and fish processing, and to ensure that the nation enjoys the benefit of the dividends from utilisation of the fisheries resources. The adoption of the legislation was very much driven by the political will to meet the public claim to the fisheries resources, both in terms of ownership and benefits that arise from them.[26]

be extracted from the earth, whether in solid, liquid, or gaseous form. Examples are groundwater and geothermal energy. The Act also covers surveys of hydropower for the generation of electricity (Article 1). The Act does not establish the concept of public ownership or property, only stating that public land in the Act means all land outside private land. According to the Act, the land is attached ownership of, not only the right to utilise, resources in the ground, while on public land, resources in the ground are the property of the State of Iceland (Article 3). Moreover, research and utilisation of resources in the ground are subject to a licence from the National Energy Authority, which lays down requirements and procedures for research on and utilisation of ground resources that are subject to the Nature Conservation Act, for instance (Article 6).

23 See e.g.: Article 5 of the Icelandic Salmonid Fisheries Act 61/2006.

24 Act 73/1990 on Icelandic national ownership of seabed resources provides for ownership of the Icelandic state of all resources that are on or within the seabed outside netting limits and fall under sovereign rights of Iceland according to laws, both national or international.

25 Act 57/1998 on the Survey and Utilisation of Ground Resources.

26 Article 2 of Act 74/2012 on Fishing Fees (frumvarp til laga um veiðigjöld, þskj. 1053, 658. mál, 140. löggjafarþing 2011–2012). The current system for fees or taxes for utilisation of the fisheries resources of Iceland was introduced in 2012. As stated in the Act, the main purpose of the legislation is to ensure that inhabitants receive the dividends that arise from the utilisation of the fisheries resources owned by the nation.

Previous constitutional proposals (1963–2009)

Codification of constitutional provisions on natural resources has long been on the political agenda, and a number of constitutional proposals were put forward both by the Althingi and by special bodies established for that purpose, but they were never adopted. The introduction of individual fishing quotas in 1990 was a key but not exclusive factor influencing how a formulation of such a provision developed, mirroring the political debate and desire to ensure public ownership of the fisheries resources. This section proposes a brief overview of these proposals discussed in chronological order.

1963–1983

The first ideas were introduced in the Althingi in 1963 by two members of the opposition (left parties),[27] who proposed that immovables and natural resources should only be owned by Icelanders. This was largely explained by Iceland's increasing international cooperation and agreements that could result in loss of control over immovable and natural resources. It is noteworthy that, at that time, the General Assembly of the UN had recently adopted Resolution 1803 of 14 December 1962 on permanent sovereignty over natural resources, based on the principle of a right to self-determination. The debate on natural resources reflected the concerns generated due to a 'sharp increase in the demand for raw material' after World War II and the desire of newly independent states to ensure equitable and fair exploitation arrangements concerning their natural resources.[28]

Since then, a number of proposals for a constitutional provision on natural resources have been introduced in the Althingi without being adopted. In 1977–1978, proposals by a member of the opposition (Peoples' Alliance)[29] on the ownership of natural resources were introduced in the Althingi providing that natural resources, such as marine resources and resources in upland ranges as distinct from other natural resources, would be common property of the nation. The discussion on ownership continued, and in 1983 a proposal was introduced by the Prime Minister (Independence Party) declaring that natural resources of Iceland were to be the 'joint and perpetual property of Icelanders' and could not therefore be owned by foreigners. These continued by stating national ownership over the resources

27 Frumvarp til stjórnarskipunarlaga, þskj. 450, 216. mál, 83. löggjafarþing 1962–1963. Again in 1964, 1966 and 1967. See also: the (at that time recently) adopted resolution 1803 by the General Assembly of 14 December 1962 on 'Permanent Sovereignty over Natural Resources.': www.ohchr.org/Documents/ProfessionalInterest/resources.pdf

28 Nico Schrijver, *Sovereignty over Natural Resources – Balancing Rights and Duties* (Cambridge University Press 2008) 4–5, 36.

29 Frumvarp til stjórnarskipunarlaga, þskj. 101, 91. mál, 98. löggjafarþing 1976–1977 and frumvarp til stjórnarskipunarlaga, þskj. 37, 36. mál, 99. löggjafarþing 1977–1978. See also: 1970 proposal by members of the People's Alliance Party: frumvarp til stjórnarskipunarlaga, þskj. 74, 72. mál, 91. löggjafarþing 1970–1971.

of the ocean and the seabed, while ownership of other natural resources was to be established by law, such as in relation to water.[30]

1990s

Following the introduction of a comprehensive system of individual, transferrable fisheries quotas in 1990,[31] public opinion increasingly called for extensive political and public debate on whether the fisheries resources had in fact become private property and subject to private property rights due to the permanent nature of the quota system. That is, whether the quota system established a property entitlement accorded permanently to the original quota owners.[32] A discussion on codifying public ownership of natural resources in the Constitution followed. The main purposes were to prevent authorisations (*leyfi til nýtingar náttúruauðlinda*) to use natural resources from becoming permanent and to prevent irrevocable control over natural resources or territories that should fall under national ownership.

In 1995, a proposal for a constitutional provision on ownership and resources management was put forward by the prime minister (Independence Party) in the Althingi, stating that marine stocks to be found within the marine zones that are subject to sovereign rights of Iceland are 'joint property of the nation.'[33] According to this proposal, provisions on the management and protection of these resources should be decided on in laws and regulations. The proposal presented two main views: that resources should be utilised in favour of 'the whole of the nation' and that Parliament should decide on the policy and on how natural resource management should be organised.

In 1996, the People's Alliance (which was at that time in opposition in parliament) put forward another constitutional proposal on natural resources[34] identical to the proposals it had introduced in 1985[35] and in 1976.[36] Its main focus was on ownership, declaring certain natural resources (i.e. mainly marine resources and upland ranges) to be 'common property of the nation.' It was, however, only in 1997 that the term 'sustainable use' first appeared in a proposal for a constitutional provision on natural resources introduced in the Althingi, again by the People's Alliance, which was still in opposition in the parliament.[37] In 1997 and 1998,

30 Frumvarp til stjórnarskipunarlaga, þskj. 537, 243. mál, 105. löggjafarþing 1982–1983.

31 Fisheries Management Act 38/1990, see also: 'Sustaining Iceland's Fisheries through Tradeable Quotas', OECD, Country Study 2017, Paper no. 9, 2: www.oecd.org/environment/resources/Policy-Paper-Sustaining-Iceland-fisheries-through-tradeable-quotas.pdf

32 *Erlingur Sveinn Haraldsson and Örn Snævar Sveinsson v. Iceland* (14 December 2007) Communication No. 1306/2004 CCPR/C/91/D/1306/2004, 20. The Icelandic fishing banks had already been declared by the Act on Fisheries Management in 1988 as common property of the Icelandic nation, and this was reiterated with the law that introduced the transferrable quota system in 1991.

33 Frumvarp til stjórnarskipunarlaga, þskj. 865, 457. mál, 118. löggjafarþing 1994–1995.

34 Frumvarp til stjórnarskipunarlaga, þskj. 70, 70. mál, 121. löggjafarþing 1996.

35 Frumvarp til stjórnarskipunarlaga, þskj. 129, 117. mál, 108. löggjafarþing 1985–1986.

36 Frumvarp til stjórnarskipunarlaga, þskj. 101, 91. mál, 91. löggjafarþing 1976–1977.

37 Frumvarp til stjórnarskipunarlaga, þskj. 271, 238. mál, 122. löggjafarþing 1997–1998.

members of the opposition Women's Party, joined by the Social Democrats in 1998, presented a proposal the main purpose of which was to specify the ownership of exploitable marine stocks within the Exclusive Economic Zone and to provide for their sustainable use.[38] The proposal did not, however, cover other natural resources. Again, these proposals reflected first and foremost the heated political discussion on the transferrable quota system in fisheries. They further reflected what was at that time the internationally emerging principle of sustainable use or development, which was first presented in 1987 by the Brundtland Commission and adopted at the Rio Conference in 1992.[39]

2000–2009

In 1998, the Althing elected a Committee on Natural Resources that delivered a comprehensive opinion on natural resources in 2000. The Committee was assigned the tasks of proposing a constitutional status for national ownership and defining natural resources. It drafted a provision stating that natural resources and land rights not subject to private property rights were the common property of the nation[40] and should be used in the 'most beneficial manner and on the basis of sustainable development.'[41] It further required that the dividends of the natural resources should be devoted to the conservation of resources, for research and maintenance, as well as for the prosperity for the nation in general.

In the comprehensive work of the 2000 Committee, a holistic approach was taken to formulating a provision on natural resources, paving the way for subsequent proposals on natural resources and public ownership, with the exception of the proposals introduced in the parliament in 2007 and the proposal introduced by the Constitutional Commission in its 2011 Report (discussed later). The 2007 proposal,[42] put forward by the Prime Minister (Independence Party) and the Minister for Industry and Commerce (Progressive Party), suggested that the natural resources of Iceland should be declared the property of the nation, without prejudice to the rights of individuals and legal persons[43] protected by the property rights clause in the Constitution (Article 72), and that they should be utilised for the benefit of the nation. The intention was to formulate a policy on Icelanders' sovereignty over all natural resources, irrespective of whether privately owned or not. Thus, natural resources, according to the proposal, were those that would fall under the sovereign

38 Frumvarp til stjórnarskipunarlaga, þskj. 271, 238. mál, 121. löggjafarþing 1997–1998, frumvarp til stjórnarskipunarlaga, þskj. 521, 268. mál, 122. löggjafarþing 1997–1998 and frumvarp til stjórnarskipunarlaga, þskj. 179, 174. mál, 123. löggjafarþing 1998–1999.

39 United Nations General Assembly, *Report of the World Commission on Environment and Development: Our Common Future* (United Nations General Assembly, Development and International Co-Operation: Environment, 1987)

40 Ibid. 27.

41 'Opinion of the Natural Resources Committee' (n 11) 27.

42 Frumvarp til stjórnarskipunarlaga, þskj. 1064, 683. mál, 133. löggjafarþing 2006–2007.

43 *2011 Report of the Constitutional Commission* (vol I) 245: www.stjornlagarad.is/other_files/stjornlagarad/skyrsla-stjornlaganefndar/skyrsla_stjornlaganefndar_fyrra_bindi.pdf

rights of Iceland and would be defined further by law.[44] No reference to sustainable development or sustainable use of natural resources was, however, made.

In February and October 2008, two almost identical proposals to those of the 2000 Committee were introduced in the Althingi by members of the Progressive Party (then in opposition), and[45] in March 2009, the Social Democrat Prime Minister and others[46] put forward a proposal to integrate natural resources and the environment in the same article of the Constitution.[47] All these proposals included a provision on ownership, sustainable development, and conservation for the benefit of all. Again, a different approach was taken from the 2007 proposal by bringing under public ownership those natural resources that were not subject to private property rights. It is against this background that the constitutional revision discussion on natural resources unfolded.

The 2011 Proposal for a New Constitution and 2012 Constitutional Bill

The 2011 Proposal for a New Constitution

In 2011, the Althingi appointed a Constitutional Council that was assigned the task of discussing the Report of the 2010–2011 Constitutional Commission and preparing a proposal for a revised constitution, taking into consideration the results of the National Forum held in 2010.[48] The Constitutional Commission's comprehensive Report on constitutional amendments included the issue of natural resources. The relevant provision began with a general statement that Iceland's natural resources should come under national ownership and should be utilised sustainably and for the benefit of all inhabitants.[49] The Constitutional Council, however, drafted a different proposal from that of the Constitutional Commission.[50] The 2011 provision on natural resources of the Constitutional Council reads as follows:

> **Article 34**
>
> Iceland's natural resources that are not private property shall be the joint and perpetual property of the nation. No one can acquire the natural resources, or

44 Ibid. 2.

45 Frumvarp til stjórnarskipunarlaga, þskj. 629, 385. mál, 135. löggjafarþing 2007–2008. Frumvarp til stjórnarskipunarlaga, þskj. 15, 15. mál, 136. löggjafarþing 2008–2009.

46 These included Parliamentarians Steingrímur J. Sigfússon, Birkir J. Jónsson, Guðjón A. Kristjánsson. The proposal was formally introduced by Prime Minister Jóhanna Sigurðardóttir.

47 Frumvarp til stjórnarskipunarlaga, þskj. 648, 385. mál, 136. löggjafarþing 2008–2009.

48 Website of the Constitutional Council: http://stjornlagarad.is/english/. See also: Chapter 6 by Salvör Nordal in this collection.

49 *2011 Report of the Constitutional Commission* (vol I) (n 43) 78.

50 Report of the presidium of the parliament on the proposals made by the Constitutional Council on amendments on the Constitution of the Republic of Iceland, þskj. 3, 3. mál, 140. löggjafarþing 2011–2012.

> rights connected thereto, as property or for permanent use and they may not be sold or pledged.
>
> Publicly owned natural resources include resources such as marine stocks, other resources of the ocean and its bottom within Iceland's economic zone and the sources of water and water-harnessing rights, the rights to geothermal energy and mining. The public ownership of resources below a certain depth under the earth's surface may be determined by law.
>
> In the use of natural resources, sustainable development and public interest shall be used for guidance.
>
> The public authorities, along with those using the natural resources, shall be responsible for their protection. The public authorities may, on the basis of law, issue permits for the use of natural resources or other limited public goods, against full payment and for a modest period of time in each instance. Such permits shall be issued on an equal-opportunity basis and it shall never lead to a right of ownership or irrevocable control of the natural resources.

The substance of the 2011 Proposal is similar to proposals introduced in 2008 and 2009 in the Althingi and to the proposals of the 2000 Committee on Natural Resources. The 2011 Proposal begins with a statement that resources that are to be found in Iceland's nature (Article 34, para 1), are not private property, and should be the joint and perpetual property of the nation. The Proposal differs though from those of 2000, 2008, and 2009, as it identified publicly owned natural resources as including marine stocks, other resources of the ocean and its bottom within Iceland's economic zone, the sources of water and water-harnessing rights, and the rights to geothermal energy and mining. What is understood by the concept of public ownership or publicly owned natural resources is explained in the Commentary on the 2011 Proposal[51] as being based on a long tradition and thinking as property that can never be sold or pledged, as reflected in the previous Article 4 of the Act 59/1928 on the Thingvellir National Park (no longer in force as amended by para 3 of Article 1 of Act 47/2004 on Thingvellir National Park): 'The protected area shall be under the protection of the Althing and remain the perpetual possession of the Icelandic nation. It can never be sold or pledged.'[52] A reference is also made to the provision on cultural heritage and the concept of natural resources and public ownership that should be read with similar understanding as they can never be sold or pledged.[53] Natural resources under public ownership would be shared with future generations, again limiting their use and transfer for private benefit.[54] In addition,

51 2011 *Proposal for a New Constitution of the Constitutional Council with Commentary*, 77: http://stjornlagarad.is/other_files/stjornlagarad/Frumvarp_med_skyringum.pdf

52 For the English version of Act 47/2004, see https://thingvellir.is/media/1503/act-on-the-thingvellir-national-park.pdf

53 2011 *Proposal for a New Constitution with Commentary* (n 51) 84.

54 Report of the presidium of the parliament on the proposals made by the Constitutional Council on amendments on the Constitution of the Republic of Iceland, þskj. 3, 3. mál, 140. löggjafarþing 2011–2012, pp. 46–48.

the Commentary explains what is meant by sustainable development by referring to the definition in the Gro Harlem Brundtland report.[55] Finally, the Commentary does not clarify what natural resources are referred to in relation to sustainable use, i.e. whether they include both those under public ownership and those privately owned.[56]

The 2012 Constitutional Bill

The public interest in a provision on natural resources remained significant, as reflected in the advisory referendum that took place in October 2012 on the Constitutional Council's Proposal. One of the six referendum questions set by the Althingi was on natural resources. Overall participation in the referendum was 48.9%.[57] The question was on the willingness to have a statement in the new Constitution to declare natural resources that are not privately owned as common property of the nation.[58] Of valid votes, 74% were in favour, whereas 15.2% did not vote in favour of such a provision.[59] Out of the six questions voted on in the referendum, the greatest support was for a provision on ownership of natural resources, gaining 82.9% of valid votes, whereas 17.1% voted against.[60] Other aspects of natural resources such as management and utilisation of natural resources were not addressed in the referendum.

A few weeks later in November 2012, a bill for a new constitution, with an article on natural resources similar to the 2011 Proposal for a New Constitution of the Constitutional Council, was introduced in the Althingi[61] by the majority of the Constitutional and Supervisory Committee (standing parliamentary committee). The provision reads:[62]

> **Article 34**
>
> Iceland's natural resources which are not subject to private property rights are the common and perpetual property of the nation. No one may acquire them or their attached rights for ownership or permanent use, and they may never be sold or mortgaged.

55 United Nations General Assembly, *Report of the World Commission on Environment and Development: Our Common Future* (United Nations General Assembly, Development and International Co-Operation: Environment, 1987).

56 2011 *Proposal for a New Constitution with Commentary* (n 51) 85–86.

57 Statistical Series, 2013:1, 18 April 2013: https://statice.is/media/43750/hag_130418.pdf, 2

58 'In the new Constitution, do you want natural resources that are not privately owned to be declared national property?'. Ibid. 18.

59 Ibid. 12.

60 Ibid. 13.

61 Frumvarp til stjórnarskipunarlaga, þskj. 510, 415. mál, 141. löggjafarþing 2012–2013. Vefútgáfa Alþingistíðinda, slóð (Constitutional Bill, Parliament document 415, parliamentary issue 415, parliamentary session 141, 2012–2013): www.althingi.is/altext/141/s/0510.html. For an English translation, see: www.althingi.is/pdf/ConstitutionJSAY7.pdf

62 Ibid.

> Property of the nation under para. 1 includes harvestable fish stocks, other resources of the sea and sea bed within Icelandic jurisdiction, beyond coastal waters with private rights to net-fish, water and other natural resources not subject to private property rights, such as water power, geothermal resources and minerals in public lands. On privately-owned land, the owners' rights to resources under the surface of the earth shall be confined to normal utilisation of the property.
>
> Utilisation of the resources shall be guided by sustainable development and the public interest.
>
> Government authorities, together with those who utilise the resources, are responsible for their protection. On the basis of law, government authorities may grant permits for the use or utilisation of resources, and other limited public assets, against full consideration and for a reasonable period of time. Such permits shall be granted on a non-discriminatory basis and shall never entail ownership or irrevocable control.

The Parliamentary Constitutional and Supervisory Committee proposed that 'resources not subject to private property rights would be the common and perpetual property of the nation'. Textual amendments to the 2011 Constitutional Council Proposal were made for clarity, and the Explanatory Notes to the 2012 Bill stressed that this provision is closely connected to Article 32 on cultural goods, Article 33 on nature and environment, Article 35 on information on the environment and standing, and lastly Article 13 on the right to ownership.[63] In addition, two amendments were made to the 2011 Proposal, the first one in relation to private property and the second on how to define what natural resources would fall under national ownership. The first amendment was described as rectification of the 2011 Proposal on the concept of ownership. That is to say, it was seen as necessary to make textual amendments to the Proposal of the Constitutional Council that were based on actual owners and not the rights attached to the resources. This would, for instance, mean that resources owned by the State or municipalities would be declared as falling under national ownership. Instead, the Parliamentary Committee proposed that resources not subject to private property rights would be the common and perpetual property of the nation. The second amendment related to the second paragraph on which natural resources would be understood as property of the nation and was made for the purpose of clarification with no substantive changes.[64] The third paragraph on utilisation of the resources and sustainable development was, according to the Explanatory Notes, to be understood as referring primarily to natural resources under public ownership, whereas the general provision on the sustainable use of natural goods was to be found in the provision on the environment.[65]

63 Ibid. 61.
64 Ibid. 61 and 63.
65 Ibid. 65.

The 2016 Constitutional Bill of the 2013–2016 Constitutional Committee

The government that took office in 2013 started a new phase of work on constitutional amendments based on previous proposals and international developments in constitutional affairs. An ad hoc committee (the Constitutional Committee) was established that soon came to the conclusion that it would not put forward a proposal for a whole new constitution.[66] Rather it would emphasise four main subjects: (1) transfer of state powers, (2) referendums, (3) environmental protection, and (4) natural resources.[67] This assessment was based on the 2012 referendum, i.e., the will of the voters and on what would likely gain general acceptance.

The work of the 2013–2016 Committee took particular notice of the fact that the advisory referendum in 2012 showed greatest support for ownership of natural resources and referendums. In early 2016, the Committee introduced its proposals as three new distinct articles (79, 80 and 81), respectively on the environment, natural resources, and referendums. Later in the summer, the government put forward a constitutional bill in parliament, which was in substance identical to the proposals made by the 2013–2016 Committee and which was not voted on before the anticipated election of October 2016.[68] This section discusses Article 80 which focusses on natural resources.

Article 80 of the 2016 Constitutional Bill

Article 80 reads as follows:[69]

> Iceland's natural resources belong to the Icelandic people. They shall be utilised sustainably and for the benefit of all inhabitants. The State controls and oversees the management and utilisation of these resources on behalf of the people.
>
> Natural resources and territories that are not subject to private property rights fall under national ownership. Nobody can obtain ownership or permanent utilisation in respect of these resources and territories and rights pertaining to them. These resources and territories may never be sold or pledged. The legislature and the executive hold the right to their control and disposal on behalf of the people.
>
> As a general rule, an appropriate fee shall be charged for authorisations to utilise natural resources and territories belonging to the Icelandic State or those falling under national ownership. The granting of usage authorisations shall be based on law and equality and transparency shall be respected. Such

66 See also Chapter 9 by Páll Þórhallsson in this collection.
67 Frumvarp til stjórnarskipunarlaga, þskj. 1577, 841. mál, 145. löggjafarþing 2015–2016, 2–3.
68 Ibid. 2–3.
69 Ibid.

authorisations never lead to permanent ownership or irrevocable control over natural resources or territories that fall under national ownership.

Each paragraph is discussed in turn as follows.

Article 80, paragraph 1

This is very much in line with the formulation introduced first in the 2000 Opinion of the Committee on Natural Resources and subsequent proposals addressing ownership, management, benefit sharing, and sustainable development. There is, however, an important difference in the opening statement of paragraph 1. Namely, the first paragraph of the 2016 Bill includes a reference to whom the natural resources of Iceland belong, along with management and utilisation. The Explanatory Notes to the Bill emphasise that the opening statement is not to be understood as referring to property rights, as such resources could be privately or publicly owned; instead, the statement is to be understood as indicating that natural resources are goods that are in the common interest of the nation and as such have a common value to the Icelandic people. The formulation is more of a policy statement restoring ideas found in earlier proposals that are more in line with notions of sovereignty over natural resources, and differing from the 2011 and 2012 proposals.[70]

The second sentence of paragraph 1 reflects two main principles for the utilisation of natural resources. The first one relates to sustainable use, as formulated and understood in the provision on environmental protection and as defined in the Brundtland report of 1987 (see the Explanatory Notes). It is noteworthy that Article 80 differs from the proposals of 2011 and 2012, as is specifically stated in the Explanatory Notes, in that sustainable use refers to *all* natural resources, not only to those under public ownership, whereas the proposals of 2011 and 2012 were less clear about this.[71] The second principle is that natural resources' use should be for the benefit of all inhabitants (*landsmönnum*). Examples of such provisions are already to be found in some legislation on natural resources utilisation, such as in the Fisheries Management Act 116/2006 and the Ground Resources Act 57/1998. Lastly, according to this provision, the State is to oversee the utilisation and management of these resources. The Explanatory Notes foresee that the State's role in this regard has to be established by law.[72]

Article 80, paragraph 2

The second paragraph is principally concerned with establishing national ownership over resources and land rights that are not subject to private property rights,

70 See e.g.: Resolution 1803 by the UN General Assembly of 14 December 1962 on 'Permanent Sovereignty over Natural Resources', www.ohchr.org/Documents/ProfessionalInterest/resources.pdf
71 (n 67) 8.
72 Ibid.

as in the 2012 Bill. A similar approach to the 2000 Opinion is thus taken with regards what resources are under national ownership. Namely, instead of enumerating in the Constitution itself the resources to be included, the 2016 Bill leaves this to statute law considering that perspectives and approaches to what is meant by natural resources may develop over time.[73] It is stressed in the Explanatory Notes to the 2016 Bill that the 'property of the nation' falls under property rights and also that delimitation thereof is the same as in the 2000 Opinion, which again forms the basis for the 2012 Constitutional Bill.[74] At the same time, the Explanatory Notes offer a definition of national ownership as a special form of property rights, distinct from property rights of individuals and legal persons protected by Article 72 of the Constitution. A property rights approach is thus taken as public ownership entails a special form of property rights alongside traditional property rights. Resources and land rights not subject to private property rights fall under national ownership. For further explanation, it is emphasised that owners of private property rights can be both individuals and legal persons such as the State and municipalities.[75]

Paragraph 2 is a response to a general call for a constitutional provision on national ownership of natural resources. The complexity of the concept of property rights is discussed in the Explanatory Notes and as such is an integral part of how national ownership is to be interpreted. Resources would fall under public ownership for two reasons: firstly, those resources that cannot be subject to ownership as there is no defined owner of them, such as sunlight or solar energy; and secondly, resources or land rights that have been handed over to the State by a specific law as those resources that were without an owner before. Examples would be the Act 58/1998 on Public Land and the Act 73/1990 on Icelandic National Ownership of Seabed Resources.[76]

Article 80, paragraph 3

Lastly, the third paragraph includes a provision on an issue that was the object of much public debate, namely a duty to pay fees for the utilisation of national resources and territories belonging to the Icelandic State or falling under national ownership. The demand for such fees has been particularly evident with respect to fisheries resources. In 2004, a fishing fee was introduced for quota owners, in which the industry pays for access to fishing resources.[77] Such granting of usage authorisation should, according to the proposal, be based on law. In addition, such usage authorisation or agreements have to be temporary and cancellable as they can never lead to permanent ownership or irrevocable control over national resources or territories that fall under national ownership. The individual transferrable quota

73 Ibid. 8 and 11; see also: 2000 'Opinion of the Natural Resources Committee' (n 11) 27.

74 Ibid. 10.

75 Ibid. 8.

76 Ibid.

77 Stefan B. Gunnlaugsson, Dadi Kristofersson, and Sveinn Agnarsson, 'Fishing for a Fee: Resource Rent Taxation in Iceland's Fisheries' (2018) 163 *Ocean and Coastal Management* 141–150.

system, which Iceland was one of the first countries to implement,[78] has very much influenced the shaping of this provision. As previously discussed, the system has been highly criticised for being de facto a permanent transfer of fishing rights from the nation.[79] Finally, the principle of legality and equality is stressed in respect to granting of such authorisations to utilise common goods of the nation.

The 2016 Constitutional Bill in light of the 2011 Proposal and the 2012 Constitutional Bill

When comparing the proposals of 2016 with the 2011 Proposal of the Constitutional Council and in 2012 Bill of the Constitutional and Supervisory Committee of the Parliament, some differences are to be found. The most noticeable one is that the 2011 and 2012 proposals identify what resources would fall under publicly owned natural resources as discussed previously. Such identification is to be found in the Explanatory Notes and not the text of the 2016 proposal,[80] where the main resources that would fall under paragraph 2 include: (1) public land, that is land and land rights not subject to private property rights, as provided for in the Act 58/1998 on Public Land, ground resources in public land, and rights in relation to surface water on public land; (2) seabed resources; (3) hydrocarbons; and (4) exploitable marine stocks in Iceland's fisheries zone. The Explanatory Notes emphasise that the listing is important when considering the main resources that would fall under that provision. The Explanatory Notes also identify resources that may not be subject to private property rights but that may have to be managed, such as wind, radio frequency, solar energy, and genetic resources.[81] This listing is, however, not exhaustive as emphasised in the Explanatory Notes.[82] By identifying the natural resources in the Explanatory Notes and not the text of the Bill itself, a similar approach is taken to that of the 2000 Committee which suggested not to define natural resources in the Constitution. Such a provision can be more open and responsive to future interpretations and development in the understanding of what natural resources are.

Moreover and importantly, by virtue of the opening statement of the 2016 proposal that Iceland's natural resources belong to the Icelandic people and that they shall be utilised sustainably and for the benefit of all inhabitants, the ideas of the 2011 Constitutional Commission's Report are invoked to some extent. The proposals of the Commission were intended to respond to the outcome of the 2010 National Forum on the Constitution and to put forward ideas for constitutional provisions to be presented to the Constitutional Council. The 2010–2011 Constitutional Commission's proposals include an opening statement that 'nature and

78 Ibid. 141.
79 See e.g.: *Erlingur Sveinn Haraldsson and Örn Snævar Sveinsson v. Iceland* (14 December 2007) Communication No. 1306/2004 CCPR/C/91/D/1306/2004, p 20.
80 Frumvarp til stjórnarskipunarlaga, þskj. 1577, 841. mál, 145. löggjafarþing 2015–2016.
81 Ibid. 8–9.
82 Ibid. 9.

the natural resources of Iceland are unassignable public properties that must be protected, used and utilised sustainably and for the benefit of all.'[83] This formulation takes more the form of a policy statement about to whom the natural resources of Iceland belong, that is, a declaration of sovereignty and sovereign rights over natural resources. It is not necessarily a reference to property rights and it differs from the 2011 and 2012 proposals in this respect. More importantly, this formulation accommodates the principles of management and utilisation of all resources to be found in Iceland. In relation to recent developments in public debate about land and land rights, which have increasingly become subject to private ownership by non-nationals, such a policy statement can also be of particular significance.[84]

Natural resources under national ownership

Considering the proposals for a constitutional provision on natural resources that have been introduced since 1963, two approaches can be identified in relation to which natural resources would fall under national ownership. The first approach considers that natural resources such as marine resources, upland ranges, and other uninhabited areas that are not subject to private ownership, as well as water energy and geothermal energy below 100 metres, should be described as falling under public ownership. This appeared in the 1976 proposal by the People's Alliance Party.[85] Later, the 2000 Committee, as well as the 2011 and 2012 proposals, had a similar approach but also defined natural resources that are not subject to private property or private property rights as coming under public ownership.

The second approach involves adopting a policy, i.e. a declaration of sovereignty, that all natural resources in Iceland either fall under national ownership or belong to Icelanders without reference to specific form of property rights, as explained by the 2010–2011 Constitutional Commission. This was the case with the 2007 proposal, beginning with a policy declaration underpinning the importance of preserving the sovereignty of Icelanders over their natural resources. The term 'natural resources' would thus cover all resources irrespective of whether they are subject to private property rights or have no owner.[86] Similar examples are to be found in the 1983, and the 2016 proposals, with Article 80 paragraph 1 being very much rooted in the proposal of the 2010–2011 Constitutional Commission. These proposals were, however, not intended to affect property rights of individuals or legal persons.

It has to be considered whether it is necessary to move away from an emphasis on identifying which natural resources would fall under public ownership,

83 *2011 Report of the Constitutional Commission* (vol I) (n 43) 78: 'The main conclusions from the National Forum' are available in English at: www.thjodfundur2010.is/english/

84 Working Group report on ownership of farms, appointed by the Minister of Fisheries and Agriculture in 2017: 'Skýrsla starfshóps um eignarhald á bújörðum': www.stjornarradid.is/lisalib/getfile.aspx?itemid=a53f6e75-c328-11e8-942c-005056bc4d74

85 Frumvarp til stjórnarskipunarlaga, þskj. 101, 91. mál, 91. löggjafarþing 1976–1977.

86 Frumvarp til stjórnarskipunarlaga, þskj. 1064, 683. mál, 133. löggjafarþing 2006–2007, p. 2.

and, consequently, from the academic debate about public ownership of natural resources and property law. It also has to be considered whether a better solution might be to declare that all of Iceland's natural resources should fall under national ownership or belong to the Icelandic people and should be used sustainably, irrespective of ownership. In fact, it can be argued that the first paragraph of the 2016 proposal combines most of what is provided for in paragraphs 2 and 3. Management and utilisation of natural resources based on principles of sustainability have economic, environmental, and social significance. Using natural resources for the benefit of all relates to the social dimension of sustainable use as well as principles of good governance. A constitutional provision that is too comprehensive and responsive to contemporary ideas and political and public debate about how and what needs to be codified can be questioned, as it could lack the necessary flexibility to accommodate new challenges such as unforeseen natural resources. The desirable approach might, therefore, be to simplify and formulate such a provision in a way that is appropriate to meet current and future developments, as well as unforeseen challenges relating to natural resources, both nationally and internationally. This leaves it to the legislative and executive powers to make laws and rules and oversee the management and utilisation of Iceland's natural resources, based on such principles.

Comparison with selected European Constitutions

Finally, as the 2013–2016 Constitutional Committee considered other constitutions,[87] a brief comparison of the Icelandic constitutional proposals on natural resources with European constitutions shows Iceland's innovative approach, both in its endeavour to codify a provision on natural resources as part of the constitutional revision and in its emphasis on the issue of ownership.[88]

Provisions on natural sources are to be found, for instance, in the Constitutions of Sweden and Norway, but no express declaration is made in either of them about the ownership of natural resources. Instead, they share the aim of sustainability of natural resources. Under Article 2 of the chapter on basic principles and the form of government, the Swedish Constitution places a duty on the 'public institutions to promote sustainable development leading to a good environment for present and future generations.'[89] The Norwegian Constitution provides that 'every person has the right to an environment that is conducive to health and to a natural environment whose productivity and diversity are maintained. Natural resources shall be managed on the basis of comprehensive long-term considerations which will safeguard

87 Frumvarp til stjórnarskipunarlaga, þskj. 1577, 841. mál, 145. löggjafarþing 2015–2016. See: Explanatory Notes to the 2016 Constitutional Bill, 7.

88 The Explanatory Notes to the 2016 Bill observe that constitutional provisions on natural resources are, though, more common in developing states. The constitutions of Finland and Denmark do not have provisions on natural resources.

89 Swedish Constitution: www.riksdagen.se/globalassets/07.-dokument-lagar/the-constitution-of-sweden-160628.pdf

this right for future generations as well' (Article 112).[90] The Finnish Constitution does not specifically address natural resources, but makes it obligatory for the public authorities to endeavour to guarantee for everyone the right to a healthy environment (section 20).

Examples of constitutions that have provisions on some form of State ownership of some or all natural resources can be found in Estonia and Ireland. The Estonian Constitution states that the 'natural wealth and resources are national riches which shall be used economically' (Article 5),[91] and the Irish constitution provides that 'all natural resources, including the air and all forms of potential energy' belong to the State.[92] Finally, the 2017 draft constitution of the Faroe Islands declared that natural resources not subject to private ownership should be publicly owned and utilised sustainably.[93]

Current state of play

The government adopted a plan for 2018–2025 for a revision of the Constitution that will be made in steps and include public consultation.[94] The first proposals focussed on natural resources and the environment and were published in May 2019. No major changes are made to the 2016 Bill by the 2019 proposal: it is mostly an edited version (to avoid repetition) of the 2016 text.[95]

Concluding remarks

The extensive public interest in incorporating a constitutional provision on natural resources highlights the fact that how natural resources utilisation is arranged in the future is of fundamental importance for the economy of Iceland. When considering the proposals for a new constitutional provision on natural resources, the main point of departure in political and public debate has been to establish public ownership over natural resources, with much less attention paid to resource utilisation based on sustainability. Thus, the bills that have been introduced since 1963 for a constitutional provision on natural resources all have in common the aim to establish national ownership of natural resources and of marine stocks in particular. Since the late 1990s, proposals have also been developed in the direction of accommodating international developments and obligations that relate to natural

90 Norwegian Constitution: www.stortinget.no/globalassets/pdf/english/constitutionenglish.pdf

91 Estonian Constitution: www.riigiteataja.ee/en/eli/530102013003/consolide

92 Irish Constitution: www.irishstatutebook.ie/eli/cons/en

93 A referendum was to be held on the Constitution on 25 April 2018, but it has so far not taken place: www.government.fo/en/news/news/referendum-on-faroese-constitution-to-be-held-on-25-april-2018/. Draft Constitution at https://d3b1dqw2kzexi.cloudfront.net/media/9831/uppskot-til-stj%C3%B3rnarskipan-f%C3%B8roya-til-umm%C3%A6lis-%C3%B3lavs%C3%B8ku-2017.pdf

94 See: www.stjornarradid.is/verkefni/stjornskipan-og-thjodartakn/stjornarskrain/stjornarskrarendurskodun-2018-2025/

95 Document 128/2019, published on 10 May 2019, draft constitutional provision on natural resources, Prime Minister's Office, https://samradsgatt.island.is/oll-mal/$Cases/Details/?id=1387

resources, especially their utilisation and preservation in the spirit of the principle of sustainable development.

Public opinion and political discussion about the need to introduce a new constitutional provision on natural resources have primarily been driven by the desire to ensure public control and equal benefit to all from the fisheries resources. At the same time, administrative implementation has been predominant in the change in natural resources law over the last decades with less emphasis on property rights.[96] The focus on ownership therefore has arguably been to the detriment of a much needed discussion of, and general consensus on, standards of management and utilisation of natural resources and on the need to codify a constitutional provision to that end.

This chapter has discussed the provision on natural resources of the 2016 Constitutional Bill in light of earlier proposals, particularly in comparison with the 2011 Proposal of the Constitutional Council and 2012 Constitutional Bill. Firstly, the 2016 Bill differs from the 2011 Proposal and 2012 Bill in terms of not defining what natural resources are in the Constitutional Bill itself, instead it elaborates on this in the Explanatory Notes, which can be referred to for the purpose of clarification and judicial interpretation. Secondly, it has an important opening statement that natural resources belong to the people irrespective of ownership. Thirdly, the 2016 Bill does not shy away from stating in the Explanatory Notes that sustainable use applies to natural resources, irrespective of whether they are under public or private ownership.

Over the last 20 years, ideas for a constitutional provision on natural resources have very much been influenced by the comprehensive proposals of the 2000 Natural Resources Committee established by the Althing. From the great variety of proposals that have been made, the content of a constitutional provision on natural resources can be described as falling mainly under three catgeories: ownership, management and utilisation, and, lastly, benefit sharing. The ownership provision has been the most controversial, and criticism has been led by academics, primarily due to the concept of public ownership, or public property, having an unclear and vague legal status within the realm of property rights law, as the public itself cannot have ownership over property. The constitutional reform process has not therefore led to any consensus on the best approach to take, and the academic debate on how to accommodate 'national property' in property law is ongoing.[97]

96 Robert L. Fischmann, 'What Is Natural Resources Law?' (2007) *Articles by Maurer Faculty*. Paper No 197, 718: www.repository.law.indiana.edu/cgi/viewcontent.cgi?article=1197&context=facpub

97 See, for instance, the following publications on natural resources and ownership: Birgir Tjörvi Pétursson (ed), *Þjóðareign – Þýðing og áhrif stjórnarskrárákvæðis um þjóðareign á auðlindum sjávar* [National Property, Meaning and Impact of a Constitutional Provision on Public Ownership of Marine Resources] (Bókafélagið Ugla Publishing in cooperation with RES Reykjavík 2007); Davíð Þorláksson, Guðrún Gauksdóttir, Ragnar Árnason, Sigurgeir B. Kristgeirsson, Sigurður Líndal, and Björg Thorarensen, '*Nokkur sjónarmið og athugasemdir við ákvæði um*

On this basis, it is suggested that the approach and aim of a constitutional provision on natural resources have to be clear with a vision for the future. It can be argued that Article 80 paragraph 1 of the 2016 proposals, declaring that 'Iceland's natural resources belong to the Icelandic people and that they shall be utilised sustainably for the benefit of all inhabitants with state control of management and utilisation,' would, for instance, be sufficient to respond to future public and political debate on natural resources, such as sovereignty over natural resources, management and administrative measures based on sustainable development, and benefit sharing. Furthermore, bearing in mind that most of the natural resources to be found in Iceland are attached to land, and thus subject to private ownership, such a statement would be responsive to rising concerns in public debate about increasing ownership of land by non-nationals.[98]

Finally, it has to be borne in mind that the management, or utilisation of, or utilisation rights over, natural resources, are usually subject to legal restrictions, such as those regarding water, freshwater fishing rights, energy and ground resources, irrespective of whether they are publicly or privately owned. Provisions are also in place establishing important resources as common property of the Icelandic nation, such as the exploitable marine stocks of the Icelandic fishing zones.[99] Notwithstanding such provisions that take the form of, for instance, supervision, licencing, and to some extent taxes, fees, and charges, there is a lack of uniform approach in relation to the purpose and aim of natural resource management and utilisation (sustainable development, benefit sharing). A constitutional provision on natural resources with an emphasis on codifying provisions relating to management aims and responsibilities based on sustainable utilisation and other international standards for the benefit of all inhabitants, as well as principles of good governance, would be beneficial to that end.

---

eignarrétt, atvinnufrelsi og náttúruauðlindir' report for the Industrial Committee of the Parliament, 7 December 2012, www.althingi.is/altext/erindi/141/141-924.pdf; and Skúli Magnússon (n 16) 233. See also Þorgeir Örlygsson, 'Um eignarhald á landi og náttúruauðlindum,' ['About ownership of land and natural resources'] in *Afmælisrit: Gaukur Jörundsson sextugur 24. September 1994* (Bókaútgáfa Orator 1994).

98 See: 2000 Opinion of the Natural Resource Committee (n 2), 17, and 19. See also: Skúli Magnússon (n 16) 230 and 233.

99 Article 1 of the Fisheries Management Act 116/2006 at http://extwprlegs1.fao.org/docs/texts/ice3455.doc

11 Would Article 79 of the 2016 Bill make much difference?

Some considerations on the legal consequences of the proposed constitutional environmental provision

Aðalheiður Jóhannsdóttir

Introduction

Over the past three decades, the bulk of Icelandic environmental and natural resources law has undergone considerable development. The most important global and regional environmental treaties have been ratified,[1] and their principal commitments incorporated into national legislation.[2] In addition, due to Iceland's membership in the European Economic Area (EEA), the bulk of the European Union's (EU) legislation relating to pollution prevention and environmental quality[3] has, through the EEA mechanism, been incorporated into the national legal system.[4] Finally, Iceland is a party to the European Convention on Human Rights (ECHR), which was also incorporated into the Icelandic legal system.[5] Notwithstanding the preceding progress, the Icelandic Constitution still contains no environmental provision. As a result, Iceland has lagged behind what appears to be an international trend in environmental constitutionalism.

Currently, around three-quarters of national constitutions reflect some aspects of environmental constitutionalism.[6] Despite definitional ambiguities, environmental

1 Including the Convention on Wetlands of International Importance especially as Waterfowl Habitat (1971); the Convention of the Conservation of European Wildlife and Natural Habitats (1979); the United Nations Convention on the Law of the Sea (1982); the Convention on Biological Diversity (1992); the Convention for the Protection of the Marine Environment of the North-East Atlantic (1992); United Nations Framework Convention on Climate Change (1992); the Kyoto Protocol to the United Nations Framework Convention on Climate Change (1997); the Convention on Access to Information, Public Participation in Decision-Making and Access to Justice in Environmental Matters (1998); Stockholm Convention on Persistent Organic Pollutants (2001); and the Paris Agreement (2015).

2 E.g.: Act 64/1994 on Hunting and Control of Birds and Wild Mammals, Act 7/1998 on Hygiene and Pollution Control, and Act 60/2013 on Nature Conservation.

3 The EEA does not, however, include EU law relating to nature conservation.

4 E.g.: Act 106/2000 on Environmental Impact Assessment, Act 23/2006 on Right to Environmental Information, Act 55/2012 on Environmental Liability, and Regulation No. 550/2018 on Emissions from Industrial Activities and Pollution Control.

5 Act 62/1994 on the European Human Right Convention.

6 Roderic O'Gorman, 'Environmental Constitutionalism: A Comparative Study' (2017) *Transnational Environmental Law* 435.

constitutionalism is sometimes understood to include three broad categories of environmental provisions.[7] The first category consists of environmental rights, including procedural environmental rights, such as the right to information, participation, and access to justice in environmental matters;[8] the rights of the environment or of nature itself; and a substantive right of individuals to an environment of a particular quality.[9] The second category encompasses environmental duties or responsibilities placed on the state and/or individuals towards the environment.[10] The third category includes environmental principles, such as the principle of integration, which calls for governance to reflect environmental concerns.[11] In addition to the preceding, references to the environment or particular environmental values may be used as justification for circumscribing or reducing the influence of other constitutionally protected rights,[12] including private property rights.

During the 105th legislative assembly 1982–1983, a proposal for a new constitution was submitted to the Althingi.[13] Interestingly, Article 80 of that proposal contained an environmental provision which seems to have been driven by the need to strengthen the conservation of nature and natural resources and by the need to ensure the public's right to roam.[14] The proposal was not accepted by the Althingi. Had it been adopted, Iceland would have been among the first states in the world to insert an environmental provision in its Constitution.

By failing over the subsequent decades to insert environmental provisions into its current Constitution, Iceland has lagged well behind the constitutional development of some of the Nordic states, notably Finland, Norway, and Sweden. Not only do historical and cultural reasons justify taking a look at the development of these three Nordic states, but their environmental constitutional provisions were to a certain degree instrumental in the preparation of the Icelandic proposals during the 2009–2017 constitutional reform process in Iceland.[15]

7 Ibid. 437–441. See also: James R May and Erin Daly, *Global Environmental Constitutionalism* (Cambridge University Press 2015) 55–84; Erin Daly and James R May, 'Introduction. Implementing Environmental Constitutionalism' in Erin Daly and James R May (eds), *Implementing Environmental Constitutionalism: Current Global Challenges* (Cambridge University Press 2018), 1–10; and Louis J Kotzé, 'Six Constitutional Elements for Implementing Environmental Constitutionalism in the Anthropocene' in Erin Daly and James R May (eds) (ibid.) 13–33.

8 May and Daly (2015) (n 7) 76–77.

9 Ibid. 63–73.

10 Ibid. 73–76.

11 O'Gorman (n 6) 440–441.

12 Ibid.

13 Frumvarp til stjórnskipunarlaga um stjórnarskrá lýðveldisins Íslands, þingskjal 573–243. mál, 105. löggjafarþing, 1982–1983, 1–34.

14 Ibid. 10 and 33.

15 *Skýrsla forsætisnefndar um tillögur stjórnlagaráðs um breytingar á stjórnarskrá Íslands*, þingskjal 3–3. mál, 140. löggjafarþing 2011–2012, 80–85, frumvarp til stjórnarskipunarlaga um stjórnarskrá lýðveldisins Íslands, þingskjal 510–415. mál, 141. löggjafarþing 2012–2013, 113–118, and finally frumvarp til stjórnarskipunarlaga um breytingu á stjórnarskrá Íslands, nr. 33/1944, með síðari breytingum (umhverfisvernd, náttúruvernd, þjóðaratkvæðisgreiðslur), þingskjal 1577–841. mál, 145. löggjafarþing 2015–2016, 4 and 11–12.

In July 2011, the Constitutional Council appointed earlier that year completed its work and handed over to the Althingi a Proposal for a New Constitution for the Republic of Iceland.[16] The general motivation behind the 2011 Proposal was the political and social turmoil that surfaced following the 2008 financial crisis.[17] Included in the Proposal's Chapter II, Human Rights and Nature, were three rather detailed Articles (Articles 33, 34, and 35) incorporating principles on environmental protection, environmental rights, ownership of natural resources and their sustainable use.[18] According to the Proposal's Commentary, the environmental provisions were part of the general revision of the human rights provisions and were driven by public opinion on environmental and natural resources issues and by the need to strengthen the conservation and management of the environment and natural resources by equipping the Constitution with basic environmental principles.[19]

As pointed out by Björg Thorarensen, the constitutional reform process was not without setbacks.[20] In 2012, a Working Group of Legal Experts was appointed by the Althingi to review the 2011 Constitutional Council's Proposal for a New Constitution.[21] Articles 33 and 35 of the 2011 Proposal underwent some minor changes, as will be outlined in this chapter.[22] The Working Group completed its work on 12 November 2012, and a new proposal was formally submitted as a constitutional bill to the Althingi during the 141st parliamentary session of 2012–2013.[23] The 2012 Constitutional Bill was, however, not adopted. This led to a new process and, eventually, to the submission of the 2016 Constitutional Bill to the Althingi in the summer 2016,[24] including an environmental provision, Article 79, which was not

16 2011 Proposal for a New Constitution: www.stjornlagarad.is/starfid/frumvarp/ (all webpages last accessed 2 June 2020). See: Björg Thorarensen, 'The Constitutional Council. Objectives and Shortcomings of an Innovative Process' in Valur Ingimundarson, Philippe Urfalino, and Irma Erlingsdóttir (eds), *Iceland's Financial Crisis: The Politics of Blame, Protest, and Reconstruction* (Routledge 2016) 239–251.

17 Björg Thorarensen, 'The People's Contribution to Constitutional Changes. Writing, Advising or Approving? – Lessons from Iceland' in Xenophon Contiades and Alkmene Fotiadou (eds), *Participatory Constitutional Change – The People as Amenders of the Constitution* (Routledge 2017) 103–119.

18 Available in English at www.stjornlagarad.is/starfid/frumvarp/

19 2011 Proposal for a New Constitution (n 16) 39–41 and 75–90.

20 Björg Thorarensen, 'The Constitutional Council. Objectives and Shortcomings of an Innovative Process' (n 16) 239–251; and Björg Thorarensen, 'The People's Contribution to Constitutional Changes. Writing, Advising or Approving? – Lessons from Iceland' (n 17) 103–119.

21 2012 Constitutional Bill: Frumvarp til stjórnarskipunarlaga um stjórnarskrá lýðveldisins Íslands, þingskjal 510–415. mál, 141. löggjafarþing 2012–2013, 28. www.althingi.is/altext/pdf/141/s/0510.pdf

22 Ibid. 7, 113–118, and 130–134.

23 Ibid. 1–252.

24 2016 Constitutional Bill: Frumvarp til stjórnarskipunarlaga um breytingu á stjórnarskrá lýðveldisins Íslands, nr. 33/1944, með síðari breytingum (umhverfisvernd, náttúruauðlindir, þjóðaratkvæðagreiðslur), þingskjal 1577–841. mál, 145. löggjafarþing, 2015–2016, 5–12. www.althingi.is/altext/pdf/145/s/1577.pdf

ultimately adopted by the end of the interim constitutional revision process, and is under consideration in the present chapter.

Against this backdrop, this chapter addresses Article 79 (the environmental provision) of the 2016 Constitutional Bill. After a brief introductory analysis and discussion, some aspects of Article 79 will first be compared with the 2011 provisions (Articles 33 and 35) as drafted by the Constitutional Council and as modified in the 2012 Constitutional Bill and will then be compared with the Norwegian provision (Article 112); the Finnish provision (Section 20); and the environmental provisions in the Swedish Constitution (the Instrument of Government's Article 2 of Chapter 1 and Article 15 situated in Chapter 2). On this basis, some critical reflections on the possible legal consequences of the proposed constitutional environmental provision in Article 79 will be presented. These reflections indicate an inherent reluctance to fully commit to environmental constitutionalism during the process leading up to the 2016 Constitutional Bill. As a result, even if that Bill had been passed by the Althingi, Article 79 would only have succeeded in marginally strengthening the conservation and management of the environment and natural resources.

Article 79 of the 2016 Constitutional Bill

Articles 33 and 35 of the 2011 Constitutional Council's Proposal for a New Constitution are obviously the blueprint for Article 79 (2016 Constitutional Bill), which follows their formulation quite closely.[25] Had the 2016 Bill been passed, Article 79 would have been situated in Chapter VII of the 1944 Constitution, along with the principal human rights provisions.[26] It would have been placed near the end of the chapter, before the two other proposed articles of the 2016 Bill: Article 80 on natural resources and Article 81 on referendums. Situating the environmental provision in Chapter VII would seem to indicate that Article 79 contains internationally established human rights. While the Explanatory Notes to the 2016 Bill do not take a clear stand on this issue, it appears to limit the protection to what has been accepted by the European Court of Human Rights when construing ECHR's Article 2 on the right to life and Article 8 on the right to respect for private and family life.[27]

25 Ibid. 1. a. (79. gr.): '(i) Náttúra Íslands er undirstaða lífs í landinu. Ábyrgð á vernd náttúru og umhverfis hvílir sameiginlega á öllum og skal verndin grundvallast á varúðar- og langtímasjónarmiðum með sjálfbæra þróun að leiðarljósi. Stuðlað skal að því að fjölbreytni náttúrunnar sé viðhaldið og vöxtur lífríkis og viðgangur tryggður. (ii) Allir skulu njóta heilnæms umhverfis. Almenningi er heimil för um landið og dvöl þar í lögmætum tilgangi. Ganga skal vel um náttúruna og virða hagsmuni landeigenda og annarra rétthafa. Mælt skal nánar fyrir í lögum um inntak og afmörkun almannaréttar. (iii) Í lögum skal mælt fyrir um rétt almennings til upplýsinga um umhverfið og áhrif framkvæmda á það svo og til þátttöku í undirbúningi ákvarðana sem áhrif hafa á umhverfið.'

26 Ibid. 1.

27 Ibid. 4–12.

In English, Article 79 reads as follows:[28]

> Nature is the foundation of life in Iceland. Responsibility for protecting nature and the environment rests collectively on all and shall be based on precautionary and long-term considerations, with sustainable development as a guiding light. Maintenance of natural diversity and ensuring a productive and flourishing biota shall be promoted.
>
> All shall enjoy a healthy environment. The public may travel and stay on the land for legitimate purposes. Nature shall be well treated, and the interests of landowners and other right holders respected. More detailed provisions for the content and delimitation of the right to roam [*almannaréttur*] shall be made by law.
>
> Law shall prescribe the right of the public to access information on the environment and on the environmental effects of any development, and to participate in the preparation of decisions affecting the environment.

Article 79, paragraph 1

The significance of nature is stated in the first sentence of paragraph 1.[29] The Explanatory Notes indicate that this is meant to declare the importance of nature for the biota, human life, and the nation's economy, reflecting the economic and social pillars of sustainable development, the inherent value of nature, and its value for present and future generations.[30] As a strategic statement, the sentence provides valuable political guidance for both policy and law-making. However, and as further explained in this chapter, it is suggested that its legal value is otherwise rather limited.

Sentence two contains two important principles. Firstly, it lays a collective responsibility for nature and environmental protection upon all, including natural and legal persons.[31] Consequently, individuals, economic operators, and the authorities are made responsible for nature and for environmental conservation.[32] It is, however, the task of the legislature to outline the exact content of the responsibility in each case, by, inter alia, defining and describing particular obligations in positive law.[33] Secondly, the responsibility is given some substance, as protection (conservation and management) should be based on precautionary and long-term considerations, guided by sustainable development. According to the Explanatory Notes, precaution entails, inter alia, that decision-making having significant impact on the environment shall be based on the best available information and

28 Author's translation.
29 2016 Constitutional Bill (n 24) 5–6.
30 Ibid.
31 Ibid. 6.
32 Ibid.
33 Ibid.

that the environment and nature be given the benefit of any doubts and uncertainties.[34] Furthermore, it is for the legislature, and for the executive when relevant, to define, develop, and elaborate further the preceding criteria, such as which information should be gathered, how to assess uncertainty, and which measures should be taken to prevent significant negative environmental impact.[35] The reference to sustainable development – which, according to the Explanatory Notes, is viewed as an overarching principle, comprising other important principles and considerations – is meant to guide conservation and management.[36] It is obvious from the Explanatory Notes that in order to have the intended effects, sustainable development needs to be further elaborated by legislation.[37] Moreover, the reference to sustainable development is expected to influence policy-making, legislating, and the interpretation of law.[38]

It is clear from the preceding that the principles in sentence two are first and foremost strategic statements, the purpose of which is to guide Parliament in legislating and to guide the interpretation of laws. By referring to the maintenance of natural diversity and to ensuring a productive and flourishing biota, the third sentence of paragraph 1 provides a material environmental objective. The reference, according to the Explanatory Notes, is primarily tied to nature conservation, including the conservation of biological diversity and the sustainable use of its components.[39]

Article 79, paragraph 2

The paragraph contains four sentences. The first declares that all shall enjoy a healthy environment. The explanations found in the Explanatory Notes are ambiguous to whether this should be understood as the 'right' of all to a healthy environment, or whether a healthy environment is a precondition for the enjoyment of other rights, including human rights according to the European Convention on Human Rights (ECHR).[40] Although related, these two interpretations are not identical.[41] Taking into account the wording of the sentence and considering the Explanatory Notes – stating the intention not to go beyond what is guaranteed by

34 Ibid.
35 Ibid.
36 Ibid. 6–7.
37 Ibid. 7.
38 Ibid.
39 Ibid.
40 Ibid.
41 E.g.: Rebecca Bratspies, 'Do We Need a Human Right to a Healthy Environment?' (2015) 13 *Santa Clara Journal of International Law* 51–57; Bridget Lewis, 'Environmental Rights or a Right to the Environment? Exploring the Nexus between Human Rights and Environmental Protection' (2012) 8 *Macquarie Journal of International and Comparative Environmental Law* 36–47. See also: Overview of the development of human rights and environmental protection in Philippe Sands and Jacqueline Peel with Adriana Fabra and Ruth MacKenzie (eds), *Principles of International Environmental Law* (4th ed, Cambridge University Press 2018) 811–827.

the right to life under Article 2 ECHR and Article 71[42] of the current Constitution[43] – the sentence does not transparently assure to all a right to a healthy environment. Rather, the intention was to ensure environmental guarantees similar to those provided by Articles 2 and 8 of the ECHR. However, no direct reference to environmental rights is to be found in Article 2, Article 8, or any other part of the ECHR. Moreover, in order to operationalise either Article 2 or Article 8 in the environmental sense, an individual interest test needs to be fulfilled.[44]

According to the second sentence, the public may travel and stay on the land for legitimate purposes, i.e. the substance of the public's right to roam is described. However, there is no mention of 'a right' to roam. Instead, the Explanatory Notes refer to the Icelandic term '*almannaréttur*,' which is a well-established and rights-oriented term in Icelandic law, although its content may have varied from time to time.[45] The meaning of the term is 'everyman's right' to access and travel through public or privately owned land and to stay there for a short period of time for legitimate purposes.[46] By inserting the content of the right to roam into Article 79, the '*almannaréttur*' would have been codified in the Constitution for the first time.[47]

The third sentence, which must be read in conjunction with the second, contains a general direction to the public on how to comport themselves when exercising their right to roam. Not only should nature be well treated, the interests of the landowner and other right holders must also be respected. As further outlined in the Explanatory Notes, the right to roam awards to the public a constitutionally protected right. This right may limit or otherwise affect the property rights of the owner of the land.[48]

The fourth and final sentence of the second paragraph addresses the legislature and stipulates that further elaboration of the content and the scope of the right to roam should be made by Acts of Parliament. Accordingly, the legislature has the discretion to elaborate the scope of the right to roam; however, any legislative elaboration must be compatible with respect for private property rights.[49]

Article 79, paragraph 3

Important procedural environmental rights are acknowledged by declaring that law should prescribe the access of the public to information on the environment

42 The provision provides guarantees similar to those of Article 8 of the ECHR. Although Iceland became a party to the ECHR in 1953, the provisions of the ECHR were not incorporated into the Icelandic legal system until the adoption of Act 62/1994 on the European Convention on Human Rights.

43 2016 Constitutional Bill (n 24) 7–8.

44 Sands, Peel, with Fabra and MacKenzie (n 41) 817–827, and in particular 819–823 and 825–826.

45 2016 Constitutional Bill (n 24) 8–9.

46 The 'almannaréttur' is currently codified in Articles 17–18 and 22 of Act 60/2013 on Nature Conservation. See further on the content and history of the right, e.g.: Aagot Vigdís Óskarsdóttir, 'Almannaréttur – frjáls för og dvöl' 1 [2015] *Úlfljótur* 104–117.

47 2016 Constitutional Bill (n 24) 8–9.

48 Ibid.

49 Ibid. 9.

and on the environmental effects of any development, and the participatory rights of the public when decisions affecting the environment are being prepared. Yet no reference to the word 'rights' in paragraph 3 actually guarantees the procedural rights mentioned, so that it is left up to the legislature to define their substance. From reading the Explanatory Notes, it is clear, nonetheless, that these rights exist and should be further elaborated by enacting legislation.[50] However, paragraph 3 makes no mention of any right of the public to have decisions affecting the environment reviewed by a higher administrative instance or by a court. This contrasts with the Explanatory Notes, which refer to existing statutory provisions on access to justice in environmental matters, albeit without giving these a constitutional status.[51] Thus the content of the paragraph 3 corresponds neither to international obligations already ratified by Iceland,[52] nor to the information contained in the Explanatory Notes.

Article 79 in the light of Articles 33 and 35 of the 2011 Proposal for a New Constitution and of the 2012 Constitutional Bill

As will be recalled, the Constitutional Council's 2011 Proposal included three environmental and natural resources articles. Two of these (Articles 33 and 35) concern environmental issues as discussed here.[53] The issue of natural resources and their sustainable use under Article 34 of the 2011 Proposal falls outside the scope of this chapter.[54] Article 33 of the 2011 Proposal for a New Constitution provides:

> **Article 33 Nature and environment of Iceland**
>
> Iceland's nature constitutes the basis for life in the country. All shall respect and protect it.
>
> All shall by law be accorded the right to a healthy environment, fresh water, unpolluted air and unspoiled nature. This means that the diversity of life and land must be maintained and nature's objects of value, uninhabited areas, vegetation and soil shall enjoy protection. Earlier damages shall be repaired as possible.
>
> The use of natural resources shall be such that their depletion will be minimised in the long term and that the right of nature and coming generations be respected.

50 Ibid.

51 Ibid. See e.g.: Act 23/2006 and Act 130/2011.

52 See: In particular the obligations in Convention on Access to Information, Public Participation in Decision-Making and Access to Justice in Environmental Matters (Aarhus Convention), which Iceland ratified and incorporated, for the greatest part, into its national legal system.

53 The English translation used here is that provided by the Constitutional Council. http://stjornlagarad.is/other_files/stjornlagarad/Frumvarp-enska.pdf (p. 8).

54 This is discussed in Chapter 10 by Ragnheiður Elfa Þorsteinsdóttir in this collection.

The right of the public to travel in the country for lawful purposes with respect for nature and the environment shall be ensured by law.

Article 35 of the 2011 Proposal provides that:

Article 35 Information on the environment and the parties concerned

The public authorities shall inform the public on the state of the environment and nature and the impact of construction thereon. The public authorities and others shall provide information on an imminent danger to nature, such as environmental pollution.

The law shall secure the right of the public to have the opportunity to participate in the preparation of decisions that have an impact on the environment and nature as well as the possibility to seek independent verdicts thereon.

In taking decisions regarding Iceland's nature and environment, the public authorities shall base their decisions on the main principles of environmental law.

Articles 33 and 35 of the 2012 Constitutional Bill are largely identical to Articles 33 and 35 of the 2011 Proposal. Two changes are worth mentioning, however. Firstly, the wording of paragraph 3 of Article 33 in the 2012 Bill – referring to the '*value* of nature and the interests of coming generations' – is slightly more anthropocentric than the text of the 2011 Proposal, which referred to 'the *right* of nature and coming generations.' Whether this particular change would have had much influence is difficult to determine. According to the Explanatory Notes to the 2012 Constitutional Bill, the reason for the change related to the wording found in International Environmental Law treaties.[55] Secondly, by adding the word 'significant' to paragraph 2 of Article 35, the participatory rights of the public were limited to particular types of environmental impact, i.e. significant impact. This change corresponds to the wording of International Environmental Law treaties, including the Aarhus Convention.

Moreover, while Articles 33 and 35 are the blueprint for the content of Article 79 of the 2016 Constitutional Bill, there are some interesting disparities, and, generally speaking, Article 79 appears to reflect weaker content than do Article 33 and 35 as presented in the 2011 Proposal. Firstly, paragraph 3 of Article 33 subjects the use of natural resources to long-term considerations respecting the value of nature and the interests of future generations,[56] and paragraph 3 of Article 35 refers to the principles of environmental law in environmental decision-making.[57] Article 79, however, in its first paragraph, refers to precautionary and long-term

55 2012 Constitutional Bill (n 21) 114–116.

56 Ibid. 114–116. The reason for the change seems to be connected to the mixed approaches in some international environmental agreements, e.g., the Convention on Biological Diversity.

57 Including the Aarhus Convention's principles, the Precautionary Principle, the Polluter Pays Principle, the Integration Principle, the Preventive Principle, and Source Principle. See further: *Skýrsla forsætisnefndar um tillögur stjórnlagaráðs um breytingar á stjórnarskrá Íslands* (n 15) 91–93; and frumvarp til stjórnarskipunarlaga um stjórnarskrá lýðveldisins Íslands (n 15) 130–134.

considerations and sustainable development, the latter only as a guiding light. No reference is made to environmental law or to its principles.[58] Secondly, the first sentence of paragraph 2 of Article 33 spells out a right to a healthy environment, including freshwater, unpolluted air, and unspoiled nature, a right that shall be accorded to all. The first sentence of paragraph 2 of Article 79 declares that all shall enjoy a healthy environment and does not in so many words award to all 'a right' to a healthy environment. Accordingly, the wording has been somewhat watered down. Despite these differences, the Explanatory Notes of both Constitutional Bills are in many ways identical, with each supporting a healthy environment as a precondition for the enjoyment of other human rights.[59] Thirdly, the reference to environmental procedural rights in paragraph 3 of Article 79 is to access to information and participation in environmental decision-making with significant impact, whereas the second paragraph of Article 35 does not qualify the participatory rights and includes access to justice. These disparities are interesting, and the 2016 Explanatory Notes do not directly clarify why the right was qualified or why access to justice was ultimately not included in the text of Article 79. However, the 2016 Explanatory Notes reflect, inter alia, how the ECHR has been construed, and they mention the Icelandic legislation incorporating the third pillar of the Aarhus Convention.[60] Fourthly, Article 79 does not place a positive duty on the authorities to inform the public on the state of the environment and nature, the impact of development thereon, or to inform the public of imminent danger to the environment. The Explanatory Notes do not directly indicate why this was left out. However, as Article 79 declares, all should enjoy a healthy environment. In light of the connection to established human rights, particularly the recent interpretations of Articles 2 and 8 of the ECHR, it is doubtful that the articulation of such a duty would make much difference to the interpretation or implementation of Article 79.[61] Finally, according to the third paragraph of Article 33, a constitutional right to roam exists and is to be guaranteed by statute, while Article 79 focussed on the core content of the right to roam and states that further content and demarcation should be elaborated by law.[62] Accordingly, due to the wording of Article 79 and as indicated in the Explanatory Notes, the legislature could delimit or reduce the right of the public to roam by enacting general legislation on the subject.[63]

58 The Explanatory Notes are silent on this issue. See: frumvarp til stjórnarskipunarlaga um breytingu á stjórnarskrá lýðveldisins Íslands, nr. 33/1944, með síðari breytingum (umhverfisvernd, náttúruauðlindir, þjóðaratkvæðagreiðslur) (n 15) 6–9 and 36–37.

59 *Skýrsla forsætisnefndar um tillögur stjórnlagaráðs um breytingar á stjórnarskrá Íslands* (n 15) 82–83. See also: frumvarp til stjórnarskipunarlaga um stjórnarskrá lýðveldisins Íslands (n 15) 36; and frumvarp til stjórnarskipunarlaga um breytingu á stjórnarskrá lýðveldisins Íslands, nr. 33/1944, með síðari breytingum (umhverfisvernd, náttúruauðlindir, þjóðaratkvæðagreiðslur) (n 15) 7–8, and 36.

60 2016 Constitutional Bill (n 24) 9.

61 Ibid. 7–8 and 36–37.

62 Ibid. 9.

63 Ibid.

Article 79 from a comparative perspective: Finland, Norway, and Sweden

Some of Iceland's Nordic neighbours, i.e. Finland, Norway, and Sweden, have inserted environmental provisions into their constitutions. In order to provide context and further understanding of Article 79, this section will briefly cover the environmental provisions of the Finnish, Norwegian, and Swedish constitutions. Parts of the environmental provisions of the constitutions of all three states appear to have influenced the development of the Icelandic provision. However, neither the jurisprudence on the Nordic provisions nor the available scholarly criticism on their effectiveness, some of which was available before 2011, seems to have been fully analysed during the Icelandic constitutional reform process.

Finland

The environmental provision of the Finnish Constitution, Section 20, came into force on 1 March 2000.[64] Its insertion was part of the Finnish constitutional transformation at the end of the twentieth century.[65] Although understood to differ from other Finnish constitutional rights[66] – including Section 7, guaranteeing the right to life, personal liberty, and integrity, and Section 10, the right to privacy – Section 20 is situated in the same chapter, Chapter 2 of the Constitution, entitled 'Basic Rights and Liberties', and has been described as a rights-based provision.[67]

Section 20 reads:

> **Responsibility for the environment**
>
> Nature and its biodiversity, the environment and the national heritage are the responsibility of everyone.
>
> The public authorities shall endeavor to guarantee for everyone the right to a healthy environment and for everyone the possibility to influence the decisions that concern their own living environment.

While the first paragraph has been described as 'soft-constitutional responsibility,'[68] the second – obliging public authorities to endeavour to guarantee everyone's right to a healthy environment and the possibility to influence decisions concerning their own living environment – is thought to create obligations on 'a more strictly

64 1999 Constitution of Finland, Act 731 as amended.

65 Juha Lavapuro, Tuomas Ojanen, and Martin Scheinin, 'Right-Based Constitutionalism in Finland and the Development of Pluralist Constitutional Review' (2011) *International Journal of Constitutional Law* 505–531.

66 According to Husa, '[T]his stipulation was deemed to underline such environmental values that are not possible to derive from the rights of individuals.' Jaakko Husa, *The Constitution of Finland: A Contextual Analysis* (Hart Publishing 2010) 194.

67 Lavapuro, Ojanen, and Scheinin (n 65) 516–517.

68 Husa (n 66), 194.

legal basis.'[69] For full effect of the second rule, the parliament would, in Jaakko Husa's view, normally enact new legislation concerning the environment.[70] This view is given considerable weight in a recent report on Finnish environmental rights.[71] It is clear from the report, which contains, inter alia, guidance on legislative reforms, that the scope of Section 20 could be better defined.[72] The report furthermore emphasises the relationship between Section 20 and other fundamental rights and its close relation to international human rights.[73] The report points out the reluctance of Finnish courts to fully engage in the development of environmental rights compared with other human rights guaranteed by the Constitution.[74] Nonetheless, Section 20 has played a part before Finnish courts, and in some recent environmental cases appealed to the Finnish Supreme Administrative Court (HFD), it has been instrumental in the interpretation of laws in environmental cases.[75] For example and not surprisingly, property rights are to be balanced against environmental rights.[76] Moreover, Section 20 has seemingly been directly applied to compensate for shortcomings in Finnish law by granting NGOs standing, contrary to a traditional interpretation of the Finnish Administrative Procedure Act.[77]

Norway

The Norwegian environmental provision, Article 112 (previously Article 110b) is situated in Section E. Human Rights of the Norwegian Constitution.[78] Inspired by, inter alia, the development of international environmental law since the early 1970s and by sustainable development policies, the environmental provision was adopted by Stortinget in 1992.[79] The two substantive elements of the provision, i.e. the right of every person to particular environmental quality (paragraph 1) and the right to environmental information pursuant to paragraph 2, remain unchanged.[80]

69 Ibid.

70 Ibid. 194–195.

71 Jukka Viljanen, Heta Heiskanen, Siina Raskulla, Timo Koivurova, and Leena Heinämäki, *Miten ympäristöperusoikeus toteutuu?* (University of Tampere Press 2014) 1–67.

72 Ibid. 3–4.

73 Ibid. 3.

74 Ibid.

75 See inter alia: HFD:2015:3, HFD:2018:1, and HFD:2018:50. See also: Husa (n 66) 195, predicting a change of paradigm within the Supreme Administrative Court.

76 See e.g.: HFD:2014:57.

77 See e.g.: HFD:2018:1.

78 English text available. www.stortinget.no/globalassets/pdf/english/constitutionenglish.pdf

79 For the development and the history of the Norwegian environmental provisions, see e.g.: Inge Lorange Backer, *Innføring i naturressurs- og miljørett* (5th edn, Gyldendal Juridisk 2012), 58–62; and Ole Kristian Fauchald, 'Hva er konsekvensene av Grunnlovens miljøparagraf?' (2015) 200 *PrivIus, Journal of Private Law*, 26–27. See also: Original Proposal and preparatory documents, www.stortinget.no/no/Saker-og-publikasjoner/Stortingsforhandlinger/Lesevisning/?p=1991-92&paid=6&wid=aIb&psid=DIVL248&pgid=aIb_0037

80 Beate Sjåfjell, 'Hvilke krav stiller Grunnloven § 112 til 'det grønne skiftet'?' (2015) 200 *Fra ord til handling. Om Grunnlovens miljøparagraf* (2015) 200 *PrivIus, Journal of Private Law* 84–90.

Paragraph 3, however, underwent some important changes in 2014,[81] as discussed here.

Article 112 contains three paragraphs:

> Every person has the right to an environment that is conducive to health and to a natural environment whose productivity and diversity are maintained. Natural resources shall be managed on the basis of comprehensive long-term considerations which will safeguard this right for future generations as well.
>
> In order to safeguard their right in accordance with the foregoing paragraph, citizens are entitled to information on the state of the natural environment and on the effects of any encroachment on nature that is planned or carried out.
>
> The authorities of the state shall issue further provisions for the implementation of these principles.

Before the 2014 constitutional amendments, the Norwegian legislature had given some thought to what would be this provision's legal effects. While not prepared to adopt a provision guaranteeing a right to environmental quality, which could be pursued in the courts by all persons, the legislature anticipated that the effects of the provision would not merely be strategic or declaratory.[82] It was commonly accepted that it was up to the authorities to choose the relevant environmental measures and that only under particular circumstances could the provision serve as an independent legal basis for substantive environmental quality.[83] It had become evident, as time went by, that the legal effects stemming from the earlier environmental provisions had been slim.[84] Therefore, in 2014, an important change was made in paragraph 3.[85] The words 'shall take measures'[86] were inserted into the paragraph in place of the words 'shall issue further provisions.'[87] Owing to its future-oriented aspect, Article 112 goes further than traditional human rights.[88] Furthermore, the Explanatory Notes are clear on the view that the environmental provision had been meant to entail legally binding obligations.[89] Due to the 1992 wording of paragraph 3, State authorities had considerable freedom in deciding whether environmental measures should be taken, and Stortinget did not rule out the possibility that the paragraph's wording

81 See further: Fauchald (n 79) 34–39.
82 E.g.: Backer (n 79) 59. See also: Fauchald (n 79) 26–27.
83 Backer (n 79) 59–62; and Fauchald (n 79), 27.
84 See further: Ole Kristian Fauchald, 'Forfatning og miljøvern – en analyse av Grunnloven § 110 b' (2007) 1–2 *Tidsskrift for rettsvitenskap* 1–84, and Fauchald (n 79) 26–34.
85 Ibid. 34–39.
86 In Norwegian: 'skal iverksette tiltak.'
87 In Norwegian: 'giver nærmere Bestemmelser.'
88 https://www.stortinget.no/globalassets/pdf/grunnlovsforslag/2011-2012/dok12-201112-031.pdf
89 Ibid.

might have contributed to the legal ineffectiveness of the environmental provision.[90] Stortinget, therefore, deemed it necessary to clarify the wording by emphasising a positive duty to take environmental measures.[91] Although some Norwegian scholars have expressed doubts as to whether the 2014 change will actually deliver the sought-after results, the duty to take measures in order to realise the rights enshrined in the first two paragraphs has been sharpened.[92]

Sweden

The Swedish Constitution contains two environmental provisions. The first, which is situated in Article 2 of Chapter 1,[93] reads as follows:

> The public institutions shall promote sustainable development leading to a good environment for present and future generations.[94]

This provision is strategic. The responsibility for the promotion of sustainable development is placed exclusively on the authorities, and Article 2 does not in so many words guarantee a right to healthy environment,[95] which is mostly operationalised by the Swedish Environmental Code ('*Miljöbalk*').[96] Nonetheless, the existence of Article 2 of Chapter 1 is considered to have some distinct legal consequences, particularly for the interpretation of law.[97] As is the case in Finland, Norway, and Iceland, Sweden is party to the ECHR, and as in the other three states, the ECHR is incorporated into the Swedish legal system.[98]

The second provision, situated in Article 15 of Chapter 2, reads as follows:

Protection of property and the right of public access

> Everyone shall have access to the natural environment in accordance with the right of public access, notwithstanding the above provisions.[99]

90 Ibid.
91 Ibid.
92 See further: Fauchald (n 79) 36–39.
93 Inserted in 2002 in the Swedish constitutional text: www.notisum.se/rnp/sls/sfs/20020903.pdf.
94 *The Constitution of Sweden: The Fundamental Laws and the Riksdag Act* (Sveriges Riksdag 2016), 65.
95 See further: Jonas Ebbesson, *Miljörätt* (Iustus förlag 2003) 100–101.
96 Miljöbalk (1998:808): http://extwprlegs1.fao.org/docs/pdf/swe50970.pdf. See also: Gabriel Michanek and Charlotta Zetterberg, *Den svenska miljörätten* (3rd ed, Iustus förlag 2012), 94–97.
97 See, inter alia: Ebbesson (n 95) 100–101.
98 Lag 1994:1219 on den europeiska konventionen angående skydd för de mänskliga rättigheterna och de grundläggande friheterna.
99 In Swedish: 'allemansrätten,' in *The Constitution of Sweden: The Fundamental Laws and the Riksdag Act* (Sveriges Riksdag 2016), 69.

The inclusion of the right of public access to nature into the Swedish Constitution seems to have been inspired by the incorporation of the ECHR into the Swedish legal system in 1994.[100] The constitutionalisation of the right of public access tempers the effects of another constitutionally protected right, namely the right to private property.[101] Although the Swedish Constitution does not define the content of the right of public access – which may vary depending on the location in Sweden[102] – the right's constitutional acknowledgement is usually viewed as being important.[103] The right is further guaranteed by the Swedish Environmental Code.[104]

Some reflections on the legal consequences of Article 79 in the 2016 Bill

The need for strengthening environmental and natural conservation in Iceland was one of the driving forces behind the development of the constitutional environmental provisions, including Article 79 of the 2016 Bill. As outlined previously, most of the environmental provisions appear to be considered to be human rights. It is, however, interesting that both the Norwegian and the Finnish provisions are thought – seemingly due to the orientation toward the future inherent in the concept of sustainable development – to differ from the environmental interpretations of the human rights guaranteed by Articles 2 and 8 of the ECHR. It is also unclear if the Swedish provision in Article 2 of Chapter 1 is viewed as a human right at all.

In contrast, Article 79 of the 2016 Constitutional Bill was not meant to provide constitutional guarantees beyond the right to life under Article 2 ECHR and the rights under Article 71 of the current Constitution (corresponding to Article 8 ECHR on the right to respect for private and family life). In this light, and as far as the right to a healthy environment and the procedural rights of Article 79 are concerned, it is questionable whether the constitutionalisation of these rights would have entailed any additional legal consequences beyond the guarantees of the current constitution.

The most notable novelty of the Icelandic proposals is perhaps the constitutional acknowledgement in Article 79 (Article 33 in the 2011 Constitutional Proposal for a New Constitution and of the 2012 Constitutional Bill) of the well established right to roam, which would have provided a constitutional guarantee of the right.

Regarding responsibility for the environment, Article 79 differs structurally from the provision found in Article 2 of Chapter 1 of the Swedish Constitution. Article 79 does, however, resemble the Finnish environmental provision in placing

100 http://data.riksdagen.se/dokument/GH01KU21

101 Ibid.

102 See: Gabriel Michanek and Charlotta Zetterberg (n 96) 201.

103 Ibid. 200–202; and Marianne Reusch, *Allemannsretten. Friluftslivets rettsgrunnlag* (Flux 2012), 60–64.

104 Miljöbalk (1998:808) (n 96).

the responsibility for environmental and nature conservation on all, including the authorities and private entities. Although it is a declaratory statement, it might have supported the legislature when deciding on conservation measures, particularly in cases where such measures might limit other constitutionally protected rights, such as private property rights.

Bearing in mind the 2014 amendments to Article 112 of the Norwegian Constitution, it is doubtful whether Article 79 would have entailed a positive duty for the legislature or the authorities to ensure the enjoyment of a healthy environment. As touched upon earlier, both Section 20 of the Finnish Constitution and Article 112 (110b) of the Norwegian Constitution have, under certain circumstances, been directly applied. The question whether individual rules of Article 79 could have been relied upon before a court of law is therefore of interest. Considering the emphasis found in the Explanatory Notes on the strategic and interpretative role of Article 79, its direct application would have been doubtful.

Reluctance to commitment to environmental constitutionalism

The aim of the present chapter has been to reflect on the legal consequences of the environmental provision (Article 79) of the Constitutional Bill of 2016. As previously mentioned, it was not adopted by the Althingi. By and large, Article 79 reflects an anthropocentric, strategic, and soft rights–based approach. Its most notable novelty would have been a constitutional acknowledgement of the public's right to roam. Although more detailed, it is evident that the environmental provisions prepared by the Constitutional Council, namely Articles 33 and 35 of the 2011 Proposal, were the blueprint for Article 79. Moreover, most of the provisions were influenced by the Finnish and Norwegian environmental constitutional provisions. However, this was seemingly done without analysing and taking on board the available scholarly criticism which, inter alia, led to the changes of the Norwegian provisions. Article 79 appears to have been intended to contain environmental human rights in line with the guarantees provided by Articles 2 and 8 of the ECHR and Article 71 of the current Constitution. This indicates a reluctance to fully commit to environmental constitutionalism. While it is unlikely that Article 79 could have been construed either as directly applicable or as placing a positive duty on the legislature to take particular and decisive measures to ensure the enjoyment of a healthy environment, there is hardly any doubt that Article 79 would have been important for the interpretation of law.

Part IV

Reflections

12 Iceland's new constitution is not solely a local concern

Thorvaldur Gylfason

Introduction

Democracy is under stress around the world. Apart from the United States, democracy was practically non-existent until 1850 when Europe was swept by revolutions that were struck down, yes, but delivered remarkable results later on. The number of democracies rose to around 25 in the interwar period, then fell to fewer than ten during the Second World War.[1] In 1943, there were only five democracies in Europe: the United Kingdom, Ireland, Iceland, Sweden, and Switzerland. From 1945 to 1960 the number of democracies rose rapidly to about 35, then stagnated during 1960–1980, and then jumped to 90, almost a half of all countries, from 1980 to 2000 after the collapse of communism around 1990. Then the spread of democracy stagnated again. There has been only a modest increase in the number of democracies since 2000.[2] A number of countries have scaled down or turned their back on democracy in recent years, including Russia and Turkey and also Thailand and Bangladesh. Autocracies are backsliding, true, but anocracies (a technical term for halfway houses between autocracy and democracy, like Russia) are increasing in number.[3] Even Hungary and Poland, fully fledged European Union members, show new signs of dwindling respect for democracy and human rights. Even the United States has been downgraded by Freedom House in its most recent reports on democracy and freedom.[4]

Against this background, the Icelandic Parliament's persistent failure since 2013[5] to ratify the Constitutional Bill supported by two-thirds of the voters in

1 The Polity Project, Global Trends in Governance 1800–2016: www.systemicpeace.org/polityproject.html. All webpages last accessed 1 June 2020.

2 Larry Diamond, 'Facing Up to the Democratic Recession' (2015) 26 *Journal of Democracy* 141. See also: The Polity Project (n 1).

3 Freedom House: https://freedomhouse.org/report/freedom-world/2019/united-states

4 Ibid.

5 During the period under review, there were three parliaments: one during 2009–2013, another during 2013–2016, and a third during 2016–2017. Political scandals, including the exposure of three Icelandic cabinet ministers in the Panama Papers, triggered elections ahead of schedule in 2016 and 2017.

the 2012 advisory referendum called by parliament is a matter of concern.[6] We should not view the challenges faced by democracy around the world at present as an excuse for disrespecting democracy in Iceland. On the contrary, we should be especially alert that now is an exceptionally inopportune time to digress from the path of democracy. When democracy is under stress as it is now even within Europe and the United States, it is of paramount importance that the Icelandic Parliament do the right thing, that it show the rest of the world that when, after the financial collapse of 2008, the people of Iceland produced perhaps the most democratic, most inclusive Constitutional Bill[7] ever made anywhere, they really meant what they did.[8] They declared their support in the 2012 referendum for using the Constitutional Council's Proposal as a 'basis for a new constitution,'[9] as well as for key individual provisions, including the articles on national ownership of natural resources[10] and equal apportionment of seats in Parliament, also known as equal suffrage or 'one person, one vote.'[11] Iceland is now in a unique position to send the rest of the world an uplifting signal about the beauty and utility of popular democracy, a signal that would be welcomed by advocates of democracy and

6 Thorvaldur Gylfason, 'Constitution Making in Action: The Case of Iceland' (2012) *VoxEU*, 1 November: https://voxeu.org/article/constitution-making-action-case-iceland.

7 An 'independent translation' of the 2011 Constitutional Bill is available on the website of the Constitutional Society (http://stjornarskrarfelagid.is/wp-content/uploads/2011/09/Iceland_New_Constitutional_Bill.pdf), as well as in print: *The New Icelandic Constitution: How Did It Come About? Where Is It?* (with a foreword by Vigdís Finnbogadóttir and introduction by Thorvaldur Gylfason) (Forlagið 2018). See also: Chapter 8 by Skúli Magnússon in this collection.

8 Further, see: Zachary Elkins, Tom Ginsburg, and James Melton (2012) 'A Review of Iceland's Draft Constitution' http://comparativeconstitutionsproject.org/wp-content/uploads/CCP-Iceland-Report.pdf (accessed 24 September 2016); Thorvaldur Gylfason, 'Constitutions: Financial Crisis Can Lead to Change' (2012) 55 *Challenge* 106–122; Thorvaldur Gylfason, 'From Collapse to Constitution: The Case of Iceland' in Luigi Paganetto (ed), *Public Debt, Global Governance and Economic Dynamism* (Springer 2013), 379–420; Anne C. M. Meuwese, 'Popular Constitution-Making. The Case of Iceland' in Denis J. Galligan and Mila Versteeg (eds), *The Social and Political Foundations of Constitutions* (Cambridge University Press 2013) 469–496; Hélène Landemore, 'Inclusive Constitution-Making: The Icelandic Experiment' (2014) *Journal of Political Philosophy*: www.academia.edu/5289629/Inclusive_Constitution-Making_the_Icelandic_Experiment; Thorvaldur Gylfason, 'Constitution on Ice' in Valur Ingimundarson, Philippe Urfalino, and Irma Erlingsdóttir (eds), *Iceland's Financial Crisis: The Politics of Blame, Protest, and Reconstruction* (Routledge 2016), 203–219; and Thorvaldur Gylfason, 'Chain of Legitimacy: Constitution Making in Iceland' in Jon Elster, Roberto Gargarella, Vatsal Naresh, and Bjørn Erik Rasch (eds), *Constituent Assemblies* (Cambridge University Press 2018) 161.

9 The first question on the ballot was: 'Do you want the proposals of the Constitutional Council to form the basis of a legislative bill for a new Constitution?' Sixty-seven per cent said Yes.

10 The second question on the ballot was: 'Would you want natural resources which are not in private ownership to be declared the property of the nation in a new Constitution?' Eighty-three per cent said Yes.

11 The fifth question on the ballot was: 'Would you want a new Constitution to include provisions to the effect that the votes of the electorate across the country should have the same force?' Sixty-seven per cent said Yes.

human rights all over the world. Parliament has neglected to send that message for five years now, from 2013 to 2017, thus inviting the rest of the world to wonder why. By 'popular democracy' here, I do not necessarily mean 'direct democracy' or 'participatory democracy.' Rather, I simply mean democracy such that politicians respect the will of the people as expressed in national referenda held by law.

The evidence that democracy is at present under stress even in Europe and America has been documented by political scientists whose recent book titles include *Democracy in America?*,[12] *How Democracies Die*,[13] and *The People vs. Democracy: Why Our Freedom Is in Danger and How to Save It*.[14] Democracy is a multifaceted phenomenon and may, therefore, mean slightly different things to different observers. One of my favourite definitions of democracy I learned from Lord George Brown, Foreign Secretary of the United Kingdom in the 1960s, who, on a visit to Reykjavík in 1971, said in private conversation: 'There shall be no one to stop us from being stupid if stupid we want to be.' By this definition, the acceptance by politicians of the results of national referenda held by law, whether they are advisory or binding, must be regarded as a sine qua non under democracy.

The 1944 Constitution

As Gudni Th. Jóhannesson, President of Iceland elected in June 2016, has described in greater detail than others, the 1944 Constitution was intended only as a provisional constitution.[15] The King of Denmark had granted Iceland its first constitution 'on the special matters of Iceland' in 1874, derived from Denmark's own constitution from 1849. The 1874 Constitution needed revision in 1920 after Iceland became a sovereign state in 1918 and again in 1944 when Iceland declared full independence from Nazi-occupied Denmark. Then the word 'King' in the text was replaced by 'President' who, importantly, would be elected directly by the nation rather than by Parliament and who would be granted certain powers, including the right to refer legislation from Parliament to national referenda, a right that, in effect, the King of Denmark had lost in 1901 when Denmark became a parliamentary monarchy.[16] Supported by Iceland's first scientific opinion poll published

12 Benjamin I. Page and Martin Gilens, *Democracy in America? What Has Gone Wrong and What We Can Do About It* (University of Chicago Press 2017).

13 Steven Levitsky and Daniel Ziblatt, *How Democracies Die* (Crown 2018).

14 Yascha Mounk, *The People vs. Democracy: Why Our Freedom is in Danger and How to Save It* (Harvard University Press 2018).

15 Guðni Th. Jóhannesson, 'Tjaldað til einnar nætur. Uppruni bráðabirgðastjórnarskrárinnar' [The Origins and Provisional Nature of Iceland's 1944 Constitution] (2012) 7 *Stjórnmál og stjórnsýsla* [Icelandic Review of Politics and Administration] 61: www.irpa.is/article/view/1116

16 Specifically, Article 26 of the 1944 Constitution states: 'If Althingi has passed a bill, it shall be submitted to the President of the Republic for confirmation not later than two weeks after it has been passed. Such confirmation gives it the force of law. If the President rejects a bill, it shall nevertheless become valid but shall, as soon as circumstances permit, be submitted to a vote by secret ballot of all those eligible to vote, for approval or rejection. The law shall become void if rejected, but

in 1943,[17] Iceland's Governor, Mr. Sveinn Björnsson,[18] was able to arrange matters such that MPs would not be granted the right to select the President.[19] This was possible because the state of play in Icelandic politics at the time had led the Governor, soon to become the country's first president, to appoint an extra-parliamentary government, in office 1942–1944. In his 1949 New Year's address to the nation, President Björnsson reminded parliament of its failure to keep its promise of a new constitution: '[W]e still have a mended garment, originally made for another country, with other concerns, a hundred years ago.'[20] He was right.

Several relatively minor changes over the years notwithstanding, the 1944 Constitution is deeply flawed, as is hardly surprising given that it dates in essence back to 1849.[21] It was perhaps fit for a nineteenth-century king but not for a modern republic. For example, the 1944 Constitution states in Article 5, 'The candidate, if there is more than one, who receives the most votes is duly elected President.' This provision would have allowed a new President to be elected with only 12% of the popular vote cast in June 2016 had each of the eight unsuccessful candidates received 11% of the vote. Luckily, that did not happen, but it could have happened. It could not, however, have happened under the new proposed constitution that parliament has thus far failed to ratify. The 2011 Constitutional Bill stipulates that the President must have majority support, ascertained through the ranking of candidates in one round of voting if desired.[22] For another example, the unequal voting

otherwise retains its force.' This important provision lay dormant from 1944 until 2004 when it was activated by President Ólafur R. Grímsson for the first time in connection with a controversial bill on news media, perceived by many as an attempt to rein in media critical of the government. The government chose to withdraw the bill rather than hold a referendum even if the Constitution does not explicitly authorise such a course of action. The provision has been employed twice since 2004, in 2010 and 2011, concerning state guarantees in connection with the Icesave dispute involving the Icelandic, British, and Dutch governments.

17 Torfi Ásgeirsson, 'Fyrsta skoðanakönnun á Íslandi' [First Opinion Poll in Iceland] (1943) No. 1–3 *Helgafell* 8–15: http://timarit.is/view_page_init.jsp?pageId=6022811

18 Following Denmark's occupation by the Nazis in 1940, Sveinn Björnsson was elected Governor of Iceland 1941–1943, in effect to serve as a substitute for the Danish King, and he was elected President 1944–1952.

19 Svanur Kristjánsson, 'Stofnun lýðveldis – Nýsköpun lýðræðis' ['Establishment of a Republic – Resurgence of Democracy'] (2002) *Skírnir*, 7; and Svanur Kristjánsson, 'Frá nýsköpun lýðræðis til óhefts flokkavalds: Fjórir forsetar Íslands 1944–1996' ['From the Creation of Democracy to Unfettered Political Party Power: Four Presidents of Iceland, 1944–1996'] (2012) *Skírnir* 50.

20 Sveinn Björnsson, 'Nýársávarp til þjóðarinnar' (New Year's Address to the Nation 1949) (author's translation): https://www.forseti.is/media/1355/010149sbnyarsavarp.pdf

21 Some of the flaws are described in Gylfason (2018) (n 8).

22 To mend this flaw, Article 78 of the 2011 Constitution Bill states: 'The President is elected by a secret ballot in a poll of all persons who have the right to vote in elections to the Althing. Presidential candidates shall have the endorsement of a minimum of one per cent and a maximum of two per cent of the electorate. Voters shall rank candidates, one or more, at their own choice in order of preference. The person who best meets the order of preference of voters, as further provided by law, is the rightfully elected President. If there is only one candidate, that candidate is duly elected without a poll being taken. In other respects, the candidacy and election of the President shall be decided by law.' The ranking of candidates secures that the office has the support of the majority of the voters, even in a single round of voting. This is a well-known property of ranked-choice voting, including instant run-off voting.

rights allowed by the 1944 Constitution produced two extra seats in parliament for the Progressives, the party of the Prime Minister after the 2013 election, and one extra seat for the Independence Party, thus giving the two parties a 60% majority in parliament even if their share of the popular vote was only 51%. This pattern was repeated in the 2016 parliamentary election in which those two parties' 40% share of the vote gave them a 46% share of the seats in parliament, though not enough to keep them in office. Both elections were held in violation of the principle of 'one person, one vote,' a principle supported by two-thirds of the voters in the 2012 national referendum on the Constitutional Council's Constitutional Bill.[23] Election observers from the Organization for Security and Co-operation in Europe (OSCE) have noted this issue in their reports. Their first priority recommendation following the 2013 parliamentary election was, 'Consideration should be given to continue the review of the legal provisions for the distribution of parliamentary seats among constituencies to ensure compliance with the principle of equal suffrage.'[24] This criticism could have been avoided had parliament ratified the Constitutional Council's Constitutional Bill.

Political dysfunction

Parliament has failed to listen to its own voice. In September 2012, parliament resolved unanimously, with 63 votes to zero and no abstentions, that 'criticism of its political culture must be taken seriously.'[25] Political culture is, in fact, quantifiable.[26] In April 2016, it came to light that the names of about 600 Icelanders, including three cabinet ministers and the First Lady,[27] were among those found in the Panama Papers.[28] Of the 332 cabinet ministers in all of Western Europe, five showed up in the Panama Papers; three of those five are Icelandic, and two of them, the leader and deputy leader of the Independence Party, remained in office as if nothing happened and ran for re-election in October 2016. So did former

23 Gylfason (2012) (n 6).

24 Organization for Security and Co-operation in Europe, Office for Democratic Institutions and Human Rights: www.osce.org/odihr/elections/iceland/103053?download=true

25 Parliamentary declaration (thingsályktunartillaga No. 29/138) on the reaction of Parliament to the report of the Special Investigation Commission (SIC) of Parliament unanimously accepted and issued on 28 September 2010. Þingsályktun um viðbrögð Alþingis við skýrslu rannsóknarnefndar Alþingis 2010: www.althingi.is/altext/138/s/1537.html

26 In an international survey of corruption perceptions, Gallup reports that 67% of Icelandic respondents consider corruption to be widespread in government in Iceland compared with 77% in the Ukraine and 15% in Denmark. See: Gallup (2013), 'Government Corruption Viewed as Pervasive Worldwide' by Jan Sonnenschein and Julie Ray: www.gallup.com/poll/165476/government-corruption-viewed-pervasive-worldwide.aspx

27 Ms. Dorrit Moussaieff was the First Lady of Iceland 2003–2016, married to President Ólafur R. Grímsson, in office 1996–2016.

28 Panama Papers, 'Politicians, Criminals and the Rogue Industry That Hides Their Cash': https://panamapapers.icij.org/

Prime Minister Mr. Sigmundur Davíð Gunnlaugsson of the Progressive Party, who resigned from office under public pressure on 5 April 2016 after the scandal broke out. All three were re-elected in October 2016. For comparison with the 600 Icelanders, there are 51 Danish names in the Panama Papers. This is not because Iceland has 12 times as many inhabitants as Denmark; as you know, it is the other way around – Denmark's population is 15 times that of Iceland.

It would take 100,000 Ukrainian names for the Ukraine to have a similar per capita presence as Iceland in the Panama Papers, but actually there are not nearly that many names listed from around the world in the leaked documents. As far as is known, it appears that about 20 Ukrainian names are listed in the Panama Papers.[29] I mention the Ukraine here for a reason. According to opinion polls, only 20% of Ukrainians say they trust the parliament in Kiev.[30] In Iceland, since the crash of 2008, polls show that an average of 15% of respondents have said they trust the Icelandic Parliament, compared with 41% on average from 1995 until the crash.[31] In early 2016, 17% expressed trust. The Icelandic people's trust in our Parliament has collapsed below even the Ukrainians' trust in their parliament in Kiev.[32] The point of this comparison is that corruption perceptions and low-quality democracy tend to go hand in hand.

These numbers appear to convey an important message. Iceland accepted economic advice and assistance from the International Monetary Fund, the Nordic countries, and Poland to resuscitate the country's economy after the crash in 2008. In many respects, the economic rescue operation orchestrated by the IMF went remarkably well. Gross national product fell by about 10% during 2009–2010 while unemployment stayed below 10% of the labour force. Thereafter, the Icelandic economy picked up steam again as a greatly depreciated domestic currency attracted foreign tourists to the country in unprecedented numbers. Thus, under the IMF's tutelage, the economic recovery from the crash was by and large successful.[33] The IMF was perhaps fortunate in that the Finance Minister who served as the IMF team's host in Iceland was Steingrímur J. Sigfússon, the leader of the Left-Green Party between 1999 and 2013. The Left-Green Party had previously, on ideological grounds, expressed hostility toward the IMF. Like Nixon in China, the Left-Greens opened Iceland's door to the IMF. However, economic recovery is not enough when a country's financial system collapses mainly due to corrupt ties between bankers and politicians, who had privatised the country's banks by

29 Ukrainian Independent Information Agency of News: www.unian.info/politics/1308200-twenty-ukrainians-exposed-in-panama-papers-leak.html

30 https://cdn-images-1.medium.com/max/800/1*WNUaqLzV7DkHwwMYGVR6uA.png

31 Capacent: https://www.gallup.is/nidurstodur/thjodarpuls/traust-til-stofnana/

32 Gallup reports an increase in trust in the Icelandic Parliament to 22% in 2017 and to 29% in 2018: https://www.gallup.is/nidurstodur/thjodarpuls/traust-til-stofnana/. For comparison, 74% of Gallup's respondents say they trust the University of Iceland.

33 Thorvaldur Gylfason, 'A Tale of Two Debtors: Iceland and Ireland – and Their Banks' (2013) *Milken Institute Review*: https://assets1b.milkeninstitute.org/assets/Publication/MIReview/PDF/14-22MR58.pdf

placing them in the hands of their cronies who took little time to bankrupt them.[34] Despite being encouraged to do so,[35] the Icelandic government between 2009 and 2013 did not receive, nor did it ask for, external assistance with amending Iceland's political and business culture. This may help to explain why Iceland is still struggling with business as usual on the political front.

The failure of Parliament to adopt the 2011 Constitutional Council's Bill needs to be viewed in this light. It is a sign of a failed political system, a failed political class that has permitted itself to stage a frontal assault on Iceland's age-old democracy. The reason for the current constitutional impasse can be found in Iceland's deficient political culture rather than in possible design flaws illuminated by constitutional theory and international experience. The ongoing impasse constitutes yet another confirmation that politicians as a rule are not fit for constitution-making, a point emphasised also by Elster (2016, 190): '[A]n ordinary legislature should not serve as a constituent assembly or as a ratifying body. In either capacity, there is risk that it might act in a self-serving manner.'[36] True, in constitutional law theory and practice, 'politicians' are rarely given the task of making or revising a constitution. Even so, this might be done by members of Parliament, but it is never with the same majority as the one required for passing ordinary legislation. In addition, constitutional changes are rarely introduced by Parliament alone and in their normal institutional configuration. Not even a simple majority in the Icelandic Parliament (a vote was not taken!) was needed to refuse to adopt the Constitutional Council's Bill after the 2012 referendum. In fact, a majority of MPs had declared in writing their support for ratification before the 2013 parliamentary election.[37]

Icelandic democracy in retrospect

Iceland has one of the oldest parliaments of the world, established almost 1100 years ago. Icelandic democracy has made impressive progress over time. In 1874 when the King of Denmark granted Iceland its Constitution, 8% of the people were eligible to vote. In 2016, 74% of the Icelandic population were registered to vote compared with 66% in the United States.[38] Voter turnout in parliamentary elections

34 Gudrun Johnsen, *Bringing Down the Banking System: Lessons from Iceland* (Palgrave MacMillan 2014); Thorvaldur Gylfason, 'Iceland: How Could This Happen?' in Torben M. Andersen, Michael Bergman, and Svend E. Hougaard Jensen (eds), *Reform Capacity and Macroeconomic Performance in the Nordic Countries* (Oxford University Press 2015) 311.

35 Thorvaldur Gylfason, 'Iceland's Special Investigation: The Plot Thickens' (2012) *VoxEU*, 30 April: https://voxeu.org/article/iceland-s-special-investigation-plot-thickens

36 Jon Elster, 'Icelandic Constitution-Making in Comparative Perspective' in Valur Ingimundarson, Philippe Urfalino, and Irma Erlingsdóttir (eds), *Iceland's Financial Crisis: The Politics of Blame, Protest, and Reconstruction* (Routledge 2016) 187–202.

37 Gylfason (2016) (n 8).

38 See: International Institute for Democracy and Electoral Assistance: www.idea.int/data-tools/data/voter-turnout. The Icelandic Constitution (Article 33) stipulates that all citizens 18 years of age or older are eligible to vote. The law on elections to Parliament (24/2000) features liberal provisions on voter registration.

in Iceland peaked at 92% in 1956 and has since gradually declined to 79% in 2016 compared with 36% in the United States in 2014.[39] The Icelandic people, with its unblemished long-standing record of liberal democracy, cannot permit its Parliament to deprive it of a new constitution that two-thirds of the voters have said they want. It is futile to argue, as some do, that the opponents of the Constitutional Council's Constitutional Bill won the 2013 parliamentary election, with 51% of the vote but 60% of the seats in Parliament.[40] If valid, such an argument would imply that politicians in Parliament can repeat elections as often as they please until they get the results they want. Only a new national referendum can overturn the results of an earlier referendum.

Why did voters, who in October 2012 expressed overwhelming support for a new constitution, turn around in April 2013 and return to power the two parties, the Independence Party and the Progressive Party, fervently against the new constitution? There appear to be two main reasons for this. First, the parliamentary election in April 2013 revolved mainly around the Progressive Party leader's promise of immediate debt relief to distressed households to be financed by squeezing foreign vulture funds that had acquired impaired assets at low prices shortly after the collapse of the banks. With three foreclosures a day on average from the crash until the 2013 election,[41] this empty promise was believed by voters who increased the Progressives' share of the vote from 15% in 2009 to 24% in 2013 and then cut it down to 12% in the 2016 election.[42] Further, in 2016, the IMF-orchestrated economic recovery since the crash may help to explain why a parliamentary election held six months ahead of schedule due to public outrage at the appearance of three of Iceland's most senior politicians in the Panama Papers nonetheless gave the Independence Party a win of two new seats in parliament.[43] Second, the literature on collective intelligence suggests that voters behave differently in different types of elections.[44] In parliamentary elections, where political parties spend large sums of money to bring their supporters to the polls, the average voter tends to enter the voting booth with the mindset of a group member or party member and to cast his or her vote accordingly. In national assemblies or referenda, where political parties

39 Statistics Iceland: https://hagstofa.is/talnaefni/ibuar/kosningar/yfirlit/

40 Statistics Iceland: http://px.hagstofa.is/pxis/pxweb/is/Ibuar/Ibuar__kosningar__althingi__althurslit/KOS02118c.px/

41 See: www.althingi.is/altext/143/s/1229.html

42 Statistics Iceland: http://px.hagstofa.is/pxis/pxweb/is/Ibuar/Ibuar__kosningar__althingi__althurslit/KOS02118b.px/

43 Constitutional Council representative Thorkell Helgason provided a useful tabulation of the results of the referendum, comparing them to an opinion poll made six months before the referendum. See: http://thorkellhelgason.is/wp-content/uploads/2012/10/S%C3%BAlurit3.pdf

44 Scott E. Page, *The Difference: How the Power of Diversity Creates Better Groups, Firms, Schools, and Societies* (new ed, Princeton University Press 2008); James Fishkin, *When the People Speak: Deliberative Democracy and Public Consultation* (Oxford University Press 2009); Hélène Landemore, *Democratic Reason: Politics, Collective Intelligence, and the Rule of the Many* (Princeton University Press 2012).

are more distant (they were virtually absent from the 2012 constitutional referendum in Iceland), the average voter is free from political party influence, casting his or her vote as a member of the community, not of a special group or party.

A fundamental rule of democracy is that election results cannot be revised; they are final, they must stand – always, without exception. Thinking and behaving otherwise amounts to an affront against democracy. That is why the results of the advisory referendum on Brexit will stand, however misguided some of us may think the outcome was. The UK will leave the EU unless perhaps Scotland mounts a successful legal challenge authorising it to exercise its veto. This is why the only correct course of action for Iceland's Parliament was to ratify the Constitutional Council's Constitutional Bill after the advisory referendum called by parliament in 2012. In the referendum,[45] an overwhelming majority of the voters (67%) declared their support for the new crowdsourced constitutional proposal as the basis for Iceland's legislation. Further, an overwhelming majority declared their support for certain key individual provisions of the new constitution. Among those provisions are the one stipulating 'one person, one vote' through equal apportionment of seats in parliament supported by 67% of the voters and the one stipulating national ownership of natural resources supported by 83% of the voters.[46] What sets those two provisions apart from the others that parliament put to the ballot in the referendum is that they concern human rights.

Human rights

Unequal voting rights have marred every parliamentary election in Iceland since 1845. In 1931, for instance, the Progressives won 55% of seats in parliament with only 35% of the votes. Even in 2013, despite modest electoral reform in stages over the years, the Progressives won 30% of the seats in parliament with 24% of the popular vote, and the Independence Party also won 30% of the seats in parliament with 27% of the popular vote.[47] Similarly, in 2016, as previously described, those two parties benefited significantly from the bias built into the electoral system through Iceland's special form of gerrymandering.[48] For example, in parliamentary elections, votes cast by those who reside at the north end of the tunnel below Hvalfjörður in Western Iceland weigh twice as heavily as

45 For the six questions on the ballot in English, see: Gylfason (2012) (n 6).

46 For detailed discussions of this provision, see: Gylfason (2013) (n 8); and 'Natural Resources as Human Rights' in David A. Carrillo (ed), *The Icelandic Federalist Papers* (Berkeley Public Policy Press 2018) chapter 15. See also: Chapter 10 by Ragnheiður Elfa Þorsteinsdóttir in this collection.

47 Statistics Iceland, Úrslit alþingiskosninga eftir kjördæmi 2013 (Results of parliamentary elections by constituency 2013): http://px.hagstofa.is/pxis/pxweb/is/Ibuar/Ibuar__kosningar__althingi__althurslit/KOS02118c.px/

48 Statistics Iceland, Úrslit alþingiskosninga eftir kjördæmi 2016 (Results of parliamentary elections by constituency 2016): http://px.hagstofa.is/pxis/pxweb/is/Ibuar/Ibuar__kosningar__althingi__althurslit/KOS02118b.px/

votes cast by those who live at the south end of the 5.8-kilometre-long tunnel. That is, the number of votes needed to elect an MP is twice as large at the south end as at the north end. Unequal suffrage has been a matter of great controversy in Iceland since the mid-nineteenth century.[49] The difference is that the 2013 and 2016 elections took place after two-thirds of the voters had declared their support for equal suffrage. Many Icelanders, recently supported by foreign election monitors from the Organization for Security and Co-operation in Europe (OSCE), view unequal voting rights on the scale observed in Iceland as a violation of their human rights.[50]

Fisheries management has been another hotly contested issue in Icelandic politics for almost 50 years.[51] The access to Iceland's fishing grounds was granted free of charge to selected vessel owners from the mid-1980s until 2002 when a nominal charge was levied on quota allocations. To make a long story short, parliament, with the stroke of a pen,[52] created a class of wealthy oligarchs – commonly referred to in Iceland as 'sea barons' and 'quota kings'[53] – by granting them free or, since 2002 (Act 85/2002), virtually free access to a common property resource which, by law, since 1990 (Act 38/1990), belongs to the people. The oligarchs, in turn – as no observer of, say, Russian politics will be surprised to hear – have used their wealth to flex their muscles in the political arena, media, and elsewhere.[54] It did not have to be that way. Norway has no oligarch to speak of. Iceland could have managed – and was indeed urged to manage – its marine resources the way that Norway manages its oil, but parliament chose not to.[55] The Constitutional Council's Constitutional Bill aims to set this right by declaring, as the law has done since 1990, that Iceland's natural resources belong to the people,[56] a polite way of stating that they do not belong to the oligarchs and that there can be no discrimination

49 Thorkell Helgason, 'Umbætur á ákvæðum um úthlutun þingsæta' [Improvements in the Apportionment of Parliamentary Seats in Iceland] (2014) 10 *Stjórnmál og stjórnsýsla* [*Icelandic Review of Politics and Administration*] 1.

50 Organization for Security and Co-operation in Europe, Office for Democratic Institutions and Human Rights: www.osce.org/odihr/elections/100321?download=true

51 Thórólfur Matthíasson, 'The Icelandic Debate on the Case for a Fishing Fee: A Non-technical Introduction' (2001) 25 *Marine Policy* 303. For legal aspects, see: David A. Carrillo (n 46).

52 The initial Fisheries Management Act (82/1983) launching the catch quota system was followed by another (38/1990) which allowed free transferability, i.e. free trade in quotas granted free of charge by the government to vessel owners. At the same time, Article 1 of the 1990 statute declares, 'Fish stocks in Icelandic waters are the common property of the Icelandic nation.'

53 In August 2018, google searches for the two terms in Icelandic ('sægreifar', 'kvótakóngar') produced 25,000 and 10,000 hits, respectively.

54 Svanur Kristjánsson, 'Varð þjóðþingið að þjófþingi? Lýðræðið og kvótakerfið 1983' ['Did Parliament Become Kleptocratic? Democracy and the Quota System 1983'] (2011) *Skírnir* 261.

55 For a brief comparison of natural resource management in Norway and Iceland, see: Thorvaldur Gylfason (2018), 'Political Economy, Mr. Churchill, and Natural Resources' (2018) 31 *Mineral Economics* 23. For more on Norway, see: Steinar Holden, 'Avoiding the Resource Curse: The Case Norway' (2013) 63 *Energy Policy* 870.

56 Article 34 of the 2011 Constitution Bill.

among citizens in the allocation of the rights to exploit these resources. This is the thrust behind the opening salvo of the preamble to 2011 constitutional proposal: 'We, the people of Iceland, wish to create a just society with equal opportunities for everyone.'[57]

The Supreme Court of Iceland, in 1998, held that the discriminatory nature of Iceland's fisheries policy regime was unconstitutional.[58] Under visible political pressure, the Supreme Court reversed course 18 months later, suddenly seeing no discrimination.[59] In 2007, the United Nations Human Rights Committee (UNHRC) confirmed the 1998 ruling and concluded in its Views that Iceland's fisheries management system is discriminatory and hence unconstitutional, a view that I consider binding de facto if not de jure.[60] Accordingly, the UNHRC instructed Iceland in 2007 to remove the discriminatory element from the system and to award damages to the two fishermen whose rights had been violated and who had brought the case before the Committee. The government of the Independence Party and the Social Democratic Alliance in office 2007–2009 did not comply with this instruction. However, its successor, comprising the Social Democrats and the Left-Greens, in office between 2009 and 2013, promised in writing in 2009 a new constitution that was underway following the financial crash and would set the matter right,[61] a promise that the Parliament has yet to keep. These events help to

57 (n 7).

58 Case No. 145/1998.

59 Case No. 12/2000. The two verdicts are discussed in Thorvaldur Gylfason, 'Sameignarauðlindir eru mannréttindi: Hvað segja lögin?' ['Common Property Resources as Human Rights: What Does the Law Say'?], *Ragnarsbók* [Festschrift for Ragnar Aðalsteinsson] (Hið íslenzka bókmenntafélag/ Mannréttindaskrifstofa Íslands [Icelandic Literary Society/Icelandic Human Rights Centre] 2009) 497–522.

60 Aðalheiður Ámundadóttir, 'Um íslenska fiskveiðistjórnunarkerfið og skyldu íslenska ríkisins til að virða álit Mannréttindanefndar Sameinuðu þjóðanna' ['On the Icelandic Fisheries Management System and the Obligation of the Icelandic State to Respect the Opinion of the United Nations Human Rights Committee'] (2008) 2 *Lögfræðingur*, 8. The UNHRC Views conclude as follows: 'The Human Rights Committee . . . is of the view that the facts before it discloses a violation of article 26 of the Covenant . . . the State party is under an obligation to provide the authors [i.e., the fishermen plaintiffs] with an effective remedy, including adequate compensation and review of its fisheries management system. . . . Bearing in mind that, by becoming a party to the Optional Protocol, the State party has recognised the competence of the Committee to determine whether there has been a violation of the Covenant or not . . . [T]he State party has undertaken to ensure to all individuals within its territory or subject to its jurisdiction the rights recognised in the 2009 Covenant and to provide an effective and enforceable remedy in case a violation has been established, the Committee wishes to receive from the State party, within 180 days, information about the measures taken to give effect to the Committee's Views.' For the full text, see: United Nations Human Rights Committee, Communication No. 1306/2004 at http://ccprcentre.org/wp-content/uploads/2012/12/1306_2004-Iceland.pdf. See also: Jakob Th. Möller and Alfred de Zayas (eds), *United Nations Human Rights Committee Case Law 1977–2008* (N. P. Engel Verlag 2009) 439–441.

61 Specifically, the Minister of Agriculture and Fisheries, Mr. Steingrímur J. Sigfússon, wrote to the UNHRC in February 2009 on behalf of the government that 'it had been decided to strengthen the human rights provisions of the Constitution and put in place a

explain why the Constitutional Bill includes a provision that aims to strengthen judicial appointments.[62]

If all the 2013–2016 parliament had done was refuse to ratify the Constitutional Council's Bill in spite of the result of the 2012 referendum, the people of Iceland would have no recourse except through their flawed electoral process that still fails to respect the principle of 'one person, one vote.' To repeat, in a democracy, a parliamentary majority cannot permit itself unilaterally to overturn the result of a constitutional referendum called by parliament, whether it was advisory or binding. As Jon Elster said on Icelandic National Television on 13 May 2012, five months before the referendum: 'If the people approved the constitutional proposal, I think parliament would find it difficult to override the moral authority of the people.'[63] The parliament, since 2013, seemingly has sought to do more. If it persists in its failure to ratify the Constitutional Council's Bill, it can be seen as trying to impede the advance of human rights by preventing the people from exercising their right to 'one person, one vote' as well as their right to the full rent generated by their natural resources that belong to them by law (Act 38/1990, Article 1). It seems inevitable that this aspect of Iceland's ongoing constitutional impasse will be brought to the attention of the UNHRC unless parliament mends its ways. In a world of globalised law and order, violations of human rights are not a local affair, not anymore.

The ongoing impasse

As if to prolong the impasse, the government in office 2013–2016 established yet another parliamentary Constitutional Committee comprising of representatives of all political parties in parliament, initially under the chairmanship of Professor Emeritus Sigurður Líndal, a steadfast opponent of constitutional reform. Over the years, several such committees have failed to produce but marginal amendments to the 1944 Constitution.[64] The mandate of the new Committee was to build a consensus across political parties by finding the lowest common denominator that all

provision to the effect that the country's marine resources are the common property of the nation' (author's translation). See: www.stjornarradid.is/efst-a-baugi/frettir/stok-frett/2012/06/05/Nidurstada-Mannrettindanefndar-STh-i-mali-nr.-1306-2004/

62 In the Constitutional Council's Bill, Article 96 on The Appointment of Public Officials states, 'When a Cabinet Minister makes an appointment to the posts of judge and Director of Public Prosecutions, the appointment shall be submitted to the President of Iceland for confirmation. If the President withholds his confirmation, the Althingi must approve the appointment by a two-thirds majority vote for the appointment to take effect.' In the past, the Minister of Justice was solely responsible for judicial appointments. It has happened that unsuccessful applicants for judgeships have been awarded damages on the grounds that they were bypassed in favour of less qualified candidates.

63 See: www.youtube.com/watch?v=IthLUGAjsdI. The quoted words begin at 3:59.

64 Since 1944, the Constitution has been amended a few times. In 1959, the Independence Party and the two left-wing parties in Parliament united against the Progressive Party to make voting rights more equal. In 1984, the number of seats in Parliament was increased to 63, effective in 1987. In 1991, Parliament was made unicameral. In 1995, modest provisions on human rights were added. In 1999, a further attempt was made to reduce the systemic rural bias of the electoral system favouring mainly the Progressive Party. Other amendments include a reduction of the minimum voting age to 20 years in 1968 and to 18 years in 1984.

Committee members could agree on as if no referendum had taken place in 2012. The Committee initially chose four provisions of the 114 in the 2011 Constitutional Bill as amended by parliament for a special speedy treatment, but after 53 meetings conducted behind closed doors over a period of three years, it came to light that those were the only four provisions considered by the Committee.[65]

One of the four provisions discussed by the Committee concerned the transfer of state powers to remove any perceived constitutional hindrance to Iceland's accession to the EU as well as to continued membership of the European Economic Area and of NATO.[66] Denmark did this in 1953, and Norway in 1962.[67] This provision was quickly taken off the table, however, suggesting that the majority of the Committee members wanted Iceland to be the sole country in Europe where EU membership is implicitly forbidden by the Constitution. This issue is of particular relevance as Iceland filed an application for EU membership in 2009 that has since been put on ice.[68] In Iceland, the majority of the parliament's

65 This is further discussed in this collection by Páll Þórhallsson (Chapter 9), and Katrín Jakobsdóttir (Chapter 13).

66 Some observers claimed at the time that Iceland's entry into the European Economic Area in 1994 violated the Constitution while others saw no conflict. A similar claim would likely be made if Iceland were to join the EU. This is why the Constitutional Council's Bill contains the following Article 111 on the Transfer of State Powers: 'International agreements involving a transfer of State powers to international organisations of which Iceland is a member in the interests of peace and economic co-operation are permitted. The transfer of State powers shall always be revocable. The meaning of transfer of State powers under an international agreement shall be further defined by law. If the Althingi approves the ratification of an agreement that involves a transfer of State powers, the decision shall be subjected to a referendum for approval or rejection. The results of such a referendum are binding.'

67 Thorvaldur Gylfason, 'The Anatomy of Constitution Making: From Denmark in 1849 to Iceland in 2017' (2017) CESifo Working Paper No. 6488, May: www.cesifo-group.de/DocDL/cesifo1_wp6488.pdf. Article 20 of Denmark's 1953 Constitution states: '(1) Powers vested in the authorities of the Realm under this Constitutional Act may, to such extent as shall be provided by statute, be delegated to international authorities set up by mutual agreement with other states for the promotion of international rules of law and cooperation. (2) For the enactment of a Bill dealing with the above, a majority of five-sixths of the members of the Folketing shall be required. If this majority is not obtained, whereas the majority required for the passing of ordinary Bills is obtained, and if the Government maintains it, the Bill shall be submitted to the electorate for approval or rejection in accordance with the rules for referenda laid down in section 42.' On Norway, see: Tom Ginsburg and James Melton (2014), 'Norway's Enduring Constitution: Implications for Countries in Transition' International Institute for Democracy and Electoral Assistance: Mahttp://comparativeconstitutionsproject.org/files/Norways_Enduring_Constitution.pdf?6c8912

68 The European Commission no longer lists Iceland among candidate countries; see: http://ec.europa.eu/environment/enlarg/candidates.htm. Even so, it is not clear that the 2013–2016 government had legal authority in 2015 to withdraw, without Parliament's approval, a membership application approved by Parliament in 2009. For this reason, it is conceivable that Iceland's application, if desired, can be quickly resuscitated in future without requiring individual approval by each member country all over again. The EU has confirmed that Iceland's application has not yet been formally withdrawn; see: https://grapevine.is/news/2015/03/19/eu-foreign-ministers-letter-doesnt-count/

Constitutional Committee members seemed to want the Constitution to prevent the people of Iceland from being able to decide freely in a national referendum about whether to join the EU. The other three provisions that the Committee could agree on are watered-down versions of the corresponding provisions in the 2011 Constitutional Bill already approved in the 2012 referendum, including the one on national ownership of natural resources.[69] In the end, the consensus of the Committee broke down. One member declared: 'The outcome [i.e., the Constitutional Committee's Proposal] is what the reactionaries [i.e., opponents of constitutional reform] can accept.'[70] The comments from the public solicited by the parliament and published on its website were overwhelmingly critical,[71] and rightly so. To repeat, the only correct course of action for parliament after the referendum was to ratify the 2011 Constitutional Bill, with or without the changes made by parliament in its November 2012 version,[72] and then to ratify it again after the 2013 election. Before the 2013 election, a majority of members of parliament had declared in writing their support for ratification, but the Speaker of Parliament failed to bring the Bill to a vote.[73] The 2009–2013 government's strategy, under the leadership of Prime Minister Jóhanna Sigurðardóttir, was to have parliament ratify the Bill before the 2013 election in the hope that parliament would ratify the Bill a second time after the election as stipulated by the 1944 Constitution (Article 79). When this strategy failed, Ms. Sigurðardóttir declared in parliament on 28 March 2013 that 'the past few weeks were the saddest period of my 35 years in Parliament.'[74]

Conclusion

In reflecting on this process, it helps to remember what the U.S. Congress did in 1787. It decided that it had no right to change the bill drafted by the Constitutional Convention in Philadelphia, not even a single word. Members of Congress understood that all that they were supposed to do was to send the bill to the 13 states for ratification. After nine states had ratified the bill, some with narrow margins, it became the law of the land without the Congress in Washington having left any

69 Gylfason (2018) (n 8). The corresponding provisions in the Constitutional Bill from 2011 are Article 34 on Natural Resources (see: n 46); Articles 33 and 35 on Iceland's Nature and Environment and Information on the Environment and Legitimate Interests; and Articles 65, 66, and 67 on Referral to the Nation, Parliamentary Business on the Initiative of Voters, and Conduct of Collections of Signatures and Referenda.

70 See: Valgerður Bjarnadóttir, 'Um stjórnarskrártillögurnar' [On the constitutional proposals] *Herðubreið* 6 March 2009: http://herdubreid.is/um-stjornarskrartillogurnar/

71 The Parliament's Constitutional Committee received 31 such comments, see: www.stjornarradid.is/verkefni/stjornskipan-og-thjodartakn/stjornarskrain/stjornarskrarnefnd-2013-2017/samrad/

72 For an English translation of the 2011 Bill, see n 7. The 2012 version does not exist in English translation.

73 These events are described further in Gylfason (2016) (n 8).

74 See: www.althingi.is/altext/raeda/141/rad20130328T015236.html (author' s translation).

fingerprints on the bill. Even so – and this is important – the process of amending the bill started almost immediately.[75]

This is what should also have happened in Iceland. Parliament should have demonstrated its respect for democracy to the Icelandic people and to the rest of the world by adopting the Constitutional Council's July 2011 Bill or parliament's November 2012 version of it, twice, i.e. before and after 2013 general elections, and then set in motion the process of amending the new constitution so adopted along the lines laid out therein with simpler rules concerning constitutional change. The simplification consists in requiring a simple majority in Parliament plus a simple majority in a national referendum for a constitutional amendment to take effect rather than requiring simple majorities in two consecutive parliaments, namely, without a national referendum as stipulated in the 1944 Constitution (Article 79).[76] If not, extra-constitutional means of ratification may have to be considered, as was done in 1944 when the new Constitution was adopted by a single parliamentary vote plus a national referendum.

It is never too late to do the right thing. It is not too late for the Icelandic Parliament to ratify the 2011/2012 Constitutional Bill. Should Parliament fail to do so, however, Iceland may stray farther toward the cluster of countries where democracy is now under the greatest stress. Iceland better not go there.

75 Pauline Maier, *Ratification: The People Debate the Constitution, 1787–1788* (Simon & Schuster 2010).

76 Article 79 of the 1944 Constitution states: 'Proposals to amend or supplement this Constitution may be introduced at regular as well as extraordinary sessions of Althingi. If the proposal is adopted, Althingi shall immediately be dissolved and a general election held. If Althingi then passes the resolution unchanged, it shall be confirmed by the President of the Republic and come into force as constitutional law.'

13 A politician's perspective

Katrín Jakobsdóttir[1]

How it all started

MPs' response to the public's demand for constitutional revision

Until the autumn of 2008, things were relatively calm on the constitutional front, and there was little discussion about the Constitution.[2] This changed with the financial collapse in October 2008, which triggered a much bigger crisis than just in the economy, as there was also a profound crisis of people's trust in public institutions, including in the Alþingi. The demand for an entirely new constitution is rooted in this; it did not originate from parliament, even though constitutional amendments had been discussed in the years 2005–2007. This demand for a new constitution came from the people taking part in the so-called pots and pans revolution. The demands were that there should be a new election, a new government, and a new constitution. Parliament tried to respond to the demand for a new constitution. At the time, I was the Minister for Education, Science and Culture and was primarily focussing on my ministry, so I had other things to attend to. However, there was a big parliamentary debate about the Constitution in the first months of 2009,[3] after the change of government in February,[4] and before the election on 25 April 2009.

1 This is an edited version of the interview that the Prime Minister gave us in her office on 25 September 2018. Katrín Jakobsdóttir originally agreed to write a chapter for this collection as a member of the 2013–2016 Constitutional Committee. When she became the Prime Minister of Iceland in November 2017, she maintained her commitment to contribute a chapter, but it was clear to us that she might no longer have the time to write it up, so we suggested an edited interview instead. Ágúst Þór and I discussed how we wanted to edit it, and I completed this work with the Prime Minister's generous involvement in checking the text and adding numerous references in footnotes. We wish to thank Skúli Magnússon for his comments on the manuscript.

2 The last constitutional revision took place in 1995, when the human rights provisions were updated and brought into line with Iceland's commitments to international human rights instruments.

3 www.althingi.is/altext/136/s/0648.html. All webpages last accessed 1 June 2020.

4 Jóhanna Sigurðardóttir, the leader of the Social Democrats, became interim Prime Minister on 1 February 2009 after the resignation of the government led by Geir Haarde (Independence Party) and a new minority government of the Social Democratic Alliance and the Left-Green Movement was formed.

The decision to create a Constitutional Assembly to draft a constitutional proposal and its aftermath

In this atmosphere of the pots and pans revolution and of lack of trust, many argued that the normal process to revise the Constitution would not work, and so it was decided in 2009 to create a special body outside parliament to draft a constitution. I think that this was an idea that was actually derived from both the Social Democratic Alliance (*Samfylking*) and the Progressive Party (*Framsóknarflokkur*).[5] The debate in the early months of 2009 revolved around issues concerning the idea of a constitutional assembly, amendments on natural resources in public ownership, protection of the environment, and national referendums. The proposal came from Jóhanna Sigurðardóttir (Social Democratic Alliance), Steingrímur J. Sigfússon (Left-Green Movement), Birkir Jón Jónsson (Progressive Party), and Guðjón Arnar Kristjánsson (Liberal Party). It was really the former opposition (Left-Green Movement, Progressive Party, and Liberal Party) and then interim Prime Minister Jóhanna Sigurðardóttir (Social Democratic Alliance) who actually proposed it on 4 March as MPs.[6] In the run-up to the early election, this heated discussion went on about constitutional change as a response to the demand for a new constitution after the crisis. There was an understanding that this demand had to be taken seriously by the Alþingi, but also there were concerns that it was important not to progress in too much haste.

The constitutional revision process formally started after the 2009 election with the adoption of Act 90/2010 on the Constitutional Assembly and the appointment of the Constitutional Commission by the Alþingi on 16 June 2010.[7] The members of this Commission were experts, and they produced good work, which was designed to serve as a basis for the Constitutional Assembly.[8] Unfortunately, however, the whole process between 2009 and 2013 soon became very problematic. It was controversial from the beginning, and the possible cost was criticised by the opposition.[9] The government wanted to keep the cost as low as possible as can be understood from the cost assessment that came with the bill itself.[10] However, the situation first became complicated when the election of the Constitutional Assembly members was challenged and annulled by the Supreme Court on 25 January 2011. As a result, the Assembly was deemed illegitimate. In retrospect, this may have been the beginning of the strained relationship between what became the Constitutional Council and the Alþingi. There had been 522 candidates in the election of the Constitutional Assembly, out of which 25 were to be elected following a new voting system, the single transferrable vote, different from the one used for the

5 On 6 February 2009, an initial bill was proposed by the Progressive Party, involving a constitutional assembly with binding power to adopt a new constitution pending a referendum: www.althingi.is/altext/136/s/0512.html
6 www.althingi.is/altext/136/s/0648.html
7 www.thjodfundur2010.is/other_files/2010/doc/Act-on-a-Constitutional-Assembly.pdf
8 This is further discussed in this collection by Björg Thorarensen (Chapter 5).
9 See e.g.: www.mbl.is/frettir/innlent/2009/03/06/stjornlagathing_fyrir_1_5_milljarda/
10 www.althingi.is/altext/138/s/0168.html

parliamentary election and introduced by Act 90/2010. So, it was chaotic, and the media complained that it was impossible to cover that election and give all the candidates the same degree of attention. There was also criticism, rightly or wrongly, that most of the Council members were 'celebrities,' while other candidates were less well known or totally unknown by the public, having less (or no) chance of being elected. So that created some frustration. There were a lot of complaints to the public broadcasting service that they were not doing enough to present all the candidates. I was the Minister for Education and Culture and thus knew of those complaints. The government's response to the Supreme Court's decision was to decide to appoint the successful candidates and formally create the Constitutional Council to replace the Constitutional Assembly.[11] But by then this had already generated a lot of difficulties. The Council started to work in April 2011, and they presented their Proposal for a New Constitution to parliament on 29 July 2011, having used the maximum time for its deliberations.[12]

This was a short time to draft a full proposal for a new constitution. Moreover, the timing was not ideal as it coincided with the summer vacation. Some of the members told me later that this made it difficult for them to obtain expert opinions. In spite of all this, the Constitutional Council delivered their Proposal for a New Constitution at the end of July.[13] A bill based on this proposal of the Constitutional Council was introduced in parliament a year later, on 16 November 2012, after the advisory referendum had been held.[14]

The decision to hold an advisory referendum

The decision to call a referendum was taken in May 2012 by the parliament, but the idea came from the Constitutional and Supervisory Committee (stjórnskipunar- og eftirlitsnefnd), the standing parliamentary committee in charge of constitutional issues. I think that the majority of MPs thought that parliament needed a clear mandate before doing more work on the Constitutional Council's Proposal and using it as the basis for a new constitution. It was therefore thought that a consultative referendum was needed to avoid a growing and deepening conflict about the Constitutional Council's appointment and role, and the majority of MPs said they needed a clear mandate. The participation rate in the referendum was just above 48%, which was nevertheless higher than expected.[15]

From parliament's perspective, the 2011 Proposal was never considered complete, so the decision was made to ask whether people wanted to build a new constitution *on the basis* of this Proposal ('Do you wish the Constitutional Council's

11 All successful candidates in the Constitutional Assembly were confirmed by the Alþingi with a 30/63 majority (with 7 abstentions, 21 votes against and 5 absents) by the Resolution of 24 March 2011: www.althingi.is/altext/139/s/1120.html

12 See Chapter 6 by Salvör Nordal in this collection.

13 http://stjornlagarad.is/english/

14 www.althingi.is/altext/141/s/0510.html

15 www.ruv.is/frett/meirihluti-sagdi-ja-vid-ollum-spurningum

Proposal to form the basis of a new draft Constitution?'). The referendum was therefore not about whether to adopt the 2011 Proposal unchanged as a new constitution, and maybe that was a complicated and a rather open question. What does it mean to build a new constitution 'on the basis of the 2011 Proposal'? I think that many people voted yes to indicate that they wanted to change the 1944 Constitution and that they wanted to use the ideas of the Constitutional Council's Proposal, but maybe not word for word. This has been an ongoing discussion ever since. What did the result of the referendum actually mean? That we were going to build on the ideas from the Constitutional Council, or did it mean that we have to use their Proposal unchanged?

In addition, the Constitutional and Supervisory Committee suggested asking five questions about specific issues, i.e. natural resources, referendums, equal weight of voting rights in all parts of the country, the status of the national Church, and whether we should implement the possibility to vote for individuals and not just political parties. I was not personally involved in this, but I think that the idea was that if we were going to hit a wall with the new constitution, we might be able to do something about these five issues. What emerged were very clear answers about the natural resources, about referendums, and about a more individualised voting system. If I recall rightly, only 38.3% did not want 'an established Church in Iceland,' but those who wanted to separate the Church from the state afterwards argued that the question had not been phrased clearly. Some 51.1% were in favour of a national Church.[16] Personally, I do not think that the question was phrased ambiguously.

At the time, there was a very strong tension between parliament and some members of the Constitutional Council who thought that the Alþingi should not be involved in drafting the revised constitution but that it should merely endorse and adopt the Constitutional Proposal as it was. This bothered many MPs, as MPs could not belong to the Constitutional Council under the Act 90/2010 establishing it, yet under the normal procedure (Article 79 of the Constitution), the revision of the Constitution is a competence of the Alþingi. In addition, it is important to recall that at that time the Alþingi and the government were facing huge challenges economically and politically. So the constitutional reform project was just one of the many issues on our agenda, along with having to rescue the state budget, avoiding national bankruptcy, and trying to deal with the Icesave crisis.[17] We also had to deal with all sorts of issues concerning Iceland's application for EU membership. We were faced with new challenges every day. As a result of all these factors, when the Constitutional Council submitted its Proposal to the Alþingi, this ongoing tension culminated in a boiling conflict about the Constitution. Looking back, the Constitutional and Supervisory Committee was really overwhelmed by the project, and they were working very hard and aiming to finish a constitutional proposal. A lot

16 www.government.is/news/article/2012/10/24/Outcome-of-the-counting-of-votes-cast-in-the-referendum-on-20-October-2012/

17 This is further discussed in this collection by Kristrún Heimisdóttir (Chapter 4).

of work still needed to be done, and late in 2012 they decided to ask the Venice Commission for an Opinion. The Draft Opinion of the Venice Commission was published on 11 February 2013,[18] and when its Final Opinion was published in March 2013,[19] the general election of 27 April was approaching fast.

No new constitution adopted, but a cross-party agreement to pursue the constitutional reform

I first really entered the discussion on the constitutional reform in February 2013 when I was elected the leader of my party, and from then on, I needed to somehow take responsibility for the constitutional reform alongside everything else. At that time, there was a growing doubt among the majority parties that adopting a new constitution in one step was the right thing to do. The opinion polls were projecting heavy losses for the government, and this gave us a clear sense of the likely results of the election, which was only weeks ahead.[20] Doubts were being voiced within the governmental parties about pushing for a new constitution, which was likely to be adopted at the end of the parliamentary term by, at best, a slim majority as opposed to a consensus. This, together with opinion polls, suggested that there would not be a majority to confirm the new constitution by the new parliament as required under Article 79 of the Constitution. This was in effect the wall that the new constitution hit at that point.[21]

Time was running out, and the Constitutional and Supervisory Committee was trying to finish its draft. It was a complicated task, and I believe they did their very best. With the election coming up in April, it dawned on us that this was becoming less and less likely, and in March the new leader of the Social Democrats actually announced that they were not going to finish their constitutional reform project.[22] This decision was probably a shock for a lot of people, and there were quite hectic meetings after that announcement. However, what we did manage to do before the election was to sign a cross-party declaration, committing all the party leaders to continuing the constitutional reform, so that all the work done since 2009 would not be lost.[23]

The 2013–2016 Constitutional Committee

After the 2013 election, the Independence Party and the Progressive Party were in government, but the Left-Green Movement, the Social Democratic Alliance, and two new parties, Bright Future and the Pirates, formed the opposition in

18 Draft Opinion No702/2013 of the Venice Commission (11 February 2013). www.venice.coe.int/webforms/documents/?pdf=CDL(2013)005-e

19 Final Opinion No702/2013 of the Venice Commission (11 March 2013). www.venice.coe.int/webforms/documents/?pdf=CDL-AD(2013)010-e

20 In the election, the Left-Green Movement lost half of its votes, and the other governmental party, the Social Democratic Alliance, lost two-thirds of their votes.

21 The 16 November 2012 Constitutional Bill (based on the 2011 Proposal for a New Constitution of the Constitutional Council) was ultimately not voted on before the end of the parliamentary term.

22 www.mbl.is/frettir/innlent/2013/03/02/klarast_ekki_a_kjortimabilinu/

23 www.mbl.is/frettir/innlent/2013/07/09/skipa_nyja_stjornarskrarnefnd/

parliament. On the basis of the cross-party agreement mentioned previously, a special committee – the Constitutional Committee – was set up to try to work on constitutional amendments.[24]

Before the election, it had been decided amongst the party leaders that this committee should focus on four issues: natural resources, referendums, the environment, and transfer of sovereignty to international organisations. In my view, the issue of the environment was very important because it had not been included in the 2012 referendum, so my own view was that it had to be part of the Constitutional Committee's remit. In relation to the transfer of sovereignty, there was a general sense in the Alþingi that this too was crucial, and the Independence Party and the Social Democrats wanted to put this on the agenda.[25] This was also considered to be crucial by the chair of the new Committee, Sigurður Líndal.[26]

Membership and lack of political leadership issues

We had decided that all the parties should be represented in the Constitutional Committee. There was one member from each of the minority parties (i.e. the Social Democrats, the Left-Greens, Bright Future, and the Pirates), but two from each of the two majority parties (i.e. the Independence Party and the Progressive Party). In addition, the Committee's chair was appointed by the Prime Minister. In my party, we decided that the constitutional revision was a very big issue which hit the wall during our time in government, and so we thought the leader of our movement had to sit on the Committee and take responsibility for this, but I was the only leader of a political party. There were a lot of problems with the membership during the work of the Committee, with some parties changing their representatives repeatedly.

In addition, except for me, the Committee's members did not really have any political mandate from their party to take any real decisions. I actually founded a group within the Left-Green Movement to continue the work on the four constitutional issues. The Committee's work went really slowly, mainly because it lacked political leadership. In my party, I had two platforms to discuss the Committee's work. One was the normal Left-Green parliamentary group: I reported to them on a regular basis and received their feedback. The other was an open grass-roots group in the party, where the people who were interested in the Constitution got together in regular meetings and via Skype and helped me formulate my opinions. Actually, now I have a new grass-roots group in my party because I think this is really important, just to have a clearer view of things and to hear what people think and want.

I know the Social Democrats also had a lot of discussions about the constitutional reform within their parliamentary group. The Pirates too had a lot of discussions about the constitutional revision in their group. What was also a decisive

24 This is further discussed in this collection by Páll Þórhallsson (Chapter 9).

25 www.ruv.is/frett/thjodaratkvaedi-um-stjornarskrarbreytingar; and www.mbl.is/frettir/innlent/2015/05/20/fagnar_bladagrein_bjarna/

26 www.ruv.is/frett/akvaedi-um-framsal-fullveldis-brynast

factor in their discussion of the constitutional revision between 2013 and 2016 is that in 2016 they had an Internet vote, asking their members whether the overall proposal should be put forward to parliament, and the majority voted no.[27] That actually made it very difficult for their representative, Aðalheiður Ámundadóttir, who had been very constructive in her work on the Constitutional Committee, to operate. Overall, I think at least three parties represented on the Committee had a lot of discussion with their members about the constitutional revision. I do not know about the other parties.

There were also some issues with the chair of the Committee. The first chairman was an elderly and respected emeritus professor of law at the University of Iceland, Sigurður Líndal, who did not come from any political party. He was directly appointed by the Prime Minister and was known to be conservative with regard to making changes to the Constitution. For many people, therefore, his appointment signalled the government's will not to pursue constitutional reform. However, in the summer 2014, he had to step down from the Committee due to health reasons. The new chairman, appointed by the Prime Minister, was Páll Þórhallsson, a good and efficient lawyer but without any political mandate. Looking back, I think it was not easy to find anyone to lead this work who had both a solid understanding of constitutional law issues and a clear political mandate. In my opinion, the reason why the Constitutional Committee did not finish its work was that it lacked political leadership. Committee members were very engaged, showed up for meetings, and sat there for hours, but the political mandate was lacking.

The difficulties faced by the Constitutional Committee showed me the importance of having a political mandate to pursue constitutional reform. This is the reason why, when my government was formed at the end of November 2017, I said I would not wish to continue with committee discussion on the constitutional reform without the involvement of all the party leaders but not their substitutes. I try to schedule the meetings so that everybody can attend, but I would not have anybody at the table who does not have a mandate to take decisions. And everybody has accepted that.

How the Constitutional Committee worked

We had about 50 meetings between 2013 and 2016, and we spent hours talking together about natural resources, the environment, referendums, and transfer of sovereignty to international institutions. We mainly used the 2011 Report of the Constitutional Commission, the 2011 Proposal of the Constitutional Council, and the 2012 Constitutional Bill put forward by the Constitutional and Supervisory Committee. So there were three basic papers to work with regarding the provisions on the environment and referendums; in relation to the constitutional status of natural resources, we also had older proposals.[28] I think that the work was quite good and

27 www.mbl.is/frettir/innlent/2016/03/11/piratar_gegn_thinglegri_medferd_tillagna/
28 These are further discussed in this collection by Ragnheiður Elfa Þorsteinsdóttir (Chapter 10).

that our 2016 proposals on natural resources, the environment, and referendums were also quite good, despite being the result of political compromise that no one was completely happy with. However, before the Committee could finish its work, we had an early election, and then politics interfered, and, of course, nobody was completely happy with the 2016 proposals as they were in effect a compromise.

The 2016 Constitutional Bill

I was not completely happy with the 2016 Bill based on the Constitutional Committee's work. I thought that the proposed constitutional provisions were pretty good, but I thought they could have been even better, had we had the time to finish our work. As I said, in summer 2016, we were faced with an unexpected election, and I think all the parties thought that they were not going to take any responsibility for bills that they were not completely happy with at that critical moment. So what happened was that new Prime Minister Sigurður Ingi Jóhannson[29] decided to present the proposals as a constitutional bill to parliament on 25 August 2016.[30] While it was clear that they were not going to be voted on, I nevertheless thought that it was correct to formally introduce these proposals to parliament as a single constitutional bill. Of course, the proposals were unfinished.

The fate of the 2016 proposals also reflects the problems involved in amending the Icelandic Constitution. Firstly, it is difficult to arrive at the consensus which is preferable, and sometimes necessary, for constitutional amendments to be passed by two separate parliaments. Secondly, since the parliament is to be dissolved after having passed a constitutional amendment in the first round, bills for constitutional reforms are submitted to the Alþing at the end of the parliamentary term. In these instances, you often have a very hectic situation in Parliament, where constitutional bills may not necessarily be the priority. This is really what happened in 2016. When you read these proposals, it is clear that they were based on ideas from the Constitutional Council, but much extra work had been put into them, not least into the Explanatory Notes to the Bill, which were good. So, if the election had been held as scheduled in April 2017, we would possibly have finished our work.

The majority of the Committee decided early on that we would not put forward a proposal on the transfer of sovereignty to international organisations. I criticised this decision because we already did so when we joined the European Economic Area in 1993. So the debate is whether we should define this transfer very narrowly – as I would like to do and include a provision about this in our Constitution – or whether it should be a broader definition or not defined at all, and this debate is ongoing. I think the Constitution needs to allow for a minimum framework by defining the limits of permissible transfer narrowly and subjecting these decisions

29 On 7 April 2016, Sigurður Ingi Jóhannson replaced Sigmundur Davíd Gunnlaugsson, who had to step down because of the so-called Panama Papers scandal.

30 Three proposed provisions were brought together under the 2016 Constitutional Bill: www.althingi.is/altext/145/s/1577.html

to proper procedures. At present, the Constitution does not explicitly allow for any transfer of sovereignty, and this has triggered scholarly criticism that we are not fully complying with the Constitution.

The proposed provision on natural resources was not what I would have put forward as the leader of the Left-Green Movement, but you may remember that we were trying to draft a bill with as much consensus as possible. However, all things considered, I think it was a proposal faithful to the guiding principle that natural resources should be in the ownership of the Icelandic people and be harvested in a sustainable way while obligating any economic operator exploiting the resources for profit to pay a normal and reasonable rent to the state. So, overall, this proposal combined a lot of different wishes. When it comes to the proposal on the environment, I would have liked to have a gone a little bit further, at least in relation to the three pillars of the Aarhus Convention: the Bill includes two of them but not the third one, that is, the public's access to justice. I thought that all three pillars should be included in our constitutional proposal. So, we had a lot of discussion within the Committee about this. I was pretty happy that the public's right to roam (almannaréttur) was actually made part of that proposal, as I think that was the most controversial aspect of this provision.

In relation to the referendums, the proposal was a compromise. The big issue was how many people you need to get to sign a petition to have a referendum, should it be 10% or 20%? The proposal settled on 15%, in addition to which there should be a threshold for participation or for agreement, which led to discussion about how high that threshold should be, and that threshold was also agreed through compromise. This is what we debated most, and I think the resulting proposal was a decent compromise. The early election was held on 29 October 2016, and, so in the end, our proposals were not voted on by the parliament.[31]

The Prime Minister and the constitutional reform: getting the job done

In 2017, new Prime Minister Bjarni Benediktsson (Independence Party, January–October) presented his idea of a holistic revision of the Constitution to be completed over three parliamentary terms. There was some opposition to this by people interested in constitutional reform, but I was positive. I would have liked to move faster, but I think this was better than not making any revisions to the Constitution. This government exploded shortly afterwards,[32] and we had a new election on 28 October 2017.

31 The window for revising the Constitution that was opened by Constitutional Act 91/2013 closed on 30 April 2017, with no change being made to the constitution. This also marked a formal end to the constitutional revision process started by the Social Democrat Prime Minister in March 2009.

32 The ruling coalition collapsed due to the decision of the Bright Future party to withdraw from it; see: *The Economist* 15 September 2017, http://country.eiu.com/article.aspx?articleid=95891993

When I became Prime Minister, I built on Bjarni Benediktsson's plan but condensed it over two parliamentary terms,[33] which is in any case the time constitutionally necessary to implement constitutional reform under Article 79. We now have party leaders at the table, and I am convinced that we will finish some important constitutional amendments. We began our discussion on the constitutional revision by focussing on the issues on which we did the most work between 2013 and 2016: natural resources, the environment, referendums, and transfer of sovereignty. Of course, we have also had a lot of discussion about how to change the Constitution. We are currently starting our discussion on amendments of the chapters on the President of the Republic and on the government. We are now entering a new stage of the constitutional revision, which is interesting for me after the 50 meetings of the Constitutional Committee.[34]

We are well aware that the process of revision itself is a sensitive issue considering that in 2011–2012 the idea had been that parliament would not involve itself too much in the reform. But I also think that the Icelandic public expects us to make progress with the constitutional revision, and we see this as essential for democracy and transparency. It is also essential for rebuilding trust in public institutions. The plan that we are following now is really modelled after the Norwegian style of changing the constitution, except they did it over a longer period. But the key is that they agreed on how they're going to do it before they started, and they have managed to change their constitution.[35] I know this was heavily criticised in Norway, but they managed to make some changes, which we have not managed to do. We tried another way between 2010 and 2017, which was innovative, but failed to deliver any changes. Therefore, since a lot of work has been done over recent years, it is now important that we should concretise some changes to the Constitution. This is particularly crucial because the criticism in Iceland now is that politicians are unable to make any constitutional changes.[36] I remember a meeting that I attended in 2016 as the representative of my party before the election in October 2016, where I was asked whether it was not just necessary to unplug Parliament completely from the constitutional revision process and to implement a new constitution without interference from Parliament. This is really the issue we are faced with. My answer to this question was no. I do not think that Parliament should or even can be cut off from the constitutional revision process, not least

33 www.stjornarradid.is/verkefni/stjornskipan-og-thjodartakn/stjornarskrain/stjornarskrarendurskodun-2018-2025/

34 'The government aims to continue with a comprehensive review of the constitution in a collaborative process involving all shades of political opinion with the involvement of the public, employing, amongst other things, methods of public consultation for this purpose. A committee on the matter will commence work at the beginning of the new parliamentary session, and the government regards it as a priority to reach a consensus on the course the work is to take.' Coalition Agreement between the Progressive Party, the Independence Party and the Left-Green, p. 32: www.stjornarradid.is/default.aspx?PageID=13c0fcaa-3869-11e6-80c7-005056bc217f

35 https://stortinget.no/en/In-English/About-the-Storting/The-Constitution/

36 This is further discussed in this collection by Thorvaldur Gylfason (Chapter 12).

because, according to our current Constitution, all constitutional amendments must go through Parliament.

I think we are actually going through times in which we see a lot of threats and challenges to democracy as well as to the role of parliaments. So I think for us sitting in parliament, it is our responsibility to face the challenge and deliver some of the constitutional amendments that we know enjoy broad support and that we and others have worked hard on for many years. However, we have to face the fact that there has never been a majority in the Alþing for the adoption of a concise new constitution. This was the political reality in 2013 but also in 2016 and in 2017. The lesson to be learned is that the best chance for constitutional reform is a step-by-step approach. Politics is about doing what is possible, and I say it is possible to reform the Constitution in this way.

Learning from the experience of 2009–2017 and looking ahead

I think the process in 2010–2013 was in many ways important. Of course, I would have preferred to see at least certain reforms coming out of this, but that is not what happened. That, however, doesn't change our obligation today to put to use all the work that was done during this period in order to move forward and ultimately deliver constitutional reforms. Some people may argue that it is not enough to make only limited and piecemeal changes: we should only settle for all or nothing! But this is ignoring reality. The 'all or nothing' approach was tried and there are numerous reasons why it did not succeed.

The lesson I learned between 2013 and 2016 is that if there is no political leadership for making constitutional reforms, then change is unlikely to happen. It is also important for politicians to resist the temptation of connecting constitutional reforms to everything else we are arguing about in politics. We must all strive for a broad consensus and build on the work that has been done before us. But while we try to bridge our differences, we must also be ready to show leadership with regard to difficult issues – like the Constitution.

In spite of economic recovery, Iceland has still not fully recovered from the moral consequences of the 2008 crisis. Given these circumstances, the public should not have to face the inability and incompetence of politicians and bureaucrats with regard to work on constitutional reforms. I also think that some of the changes are more important for the Icelandic public than others. For instance, if you were to ask the Icelandic people, you might find that the question of natural resources is one of the most important issues for a lot of them because we are a natural resource–based society.[37]

All things considered, I think it is particularly important for democracy and politics in Iceland that we now continue with our work on constitutional reforms.

37 Proposal of natural resources, put to consultation 19 June 2019. https://samradsgatt.island.is/oll-mal/$Cases/Details/?id=1387

I therefore see this as an important project, not only for me as Prime Minister and for all political parties in Iceland, but also for politics and democracy in Iceland as a whole. I think we have had a very frustrating history of 'constitutional non-changes' in the last ten years (not to go further back in time), and it is, by now, high time that the system delivers!

14 Conclusion

What has changed?

Catherine Dupré

Failure for some, success for others: assessing the overall outcome of the constitutional reform undertaken between 2009 and 2017 is a fraught process. It might not be the most helpful discussion to have either. Indeed, it is difficult to assess the Icelandic reform process that took place in that period, when there was such little consensus on its intended ultimate goal or even necessity. In addition, assessment depends on the perspective and time frame adopted by the assessor and, for instance, on whether it is short term or long term. Although it might be too soon to decide on this, it is suggested that reflecting on what has changed with the reform process might be a more informative exercise, albeit still a difficult one. On that basis, a before-and-after comparison can bring to light some important issues.

The 1944 Constitution re-imagined and rejuvenated

It is suggested that the 1944 Constitution has emerged stronger and richer from these years of reform and discussion. It was subjected to one of the toughest 'stress tests' (to use the phrase of the Constitutional Council about the 2011 Proposal for a New Constitution) that a constitution can face. This involved overcoming two major challenges. One was to safeguard Icelandic democracy and steer it through a crisis of unprecedented magnitude. The other was to allow for novel approaches involving Icelanders in constitutional reform and discussion in a wide range of ways, while remaining within the procedure of Article 79, including by adopting an interim constitutional revision procedure with Constitutional Act 91/2013.

While no change was ultimately made to the formal text of the Constitution, it may arguably no longer be viewed as a 'patched garment' (as it was for some when originally adopted); it has been rejuvenated and invigorated during those years of discussion.[1] Firstly, one of its core features, namely the power of the President under Article 26, was eventually clarified, therefore completing the construction of the Icelandic Republic and of Icelanders as a constitutional People. In addition,

1 Ming-Sung Kuo, 'Between Fact and Norm: Narrative and the Constitutionalisation of Founding Moments' in Richard Albert, Menaka Guruswamy, and Nishchal Basnyat (eds), *Founding Moments in Constitutionalism* (Hart 2019) 11, 13.

and within the reform process, the 1944 Constitution was subjected to close and comprehensive scrutiny of most (if not all) its components. As a result, it is now perceived in what could be called a holistic manner, that is as a text greater than the sum of its parts, the reform of which – even if partial – has to be considered from the perspective of the entire constitutional equilibrium and its workability. Above all perhaps, new ideas and new issues were put forward in numerous fora and in an unprecedentedly inclusive manner. Importantly too, most of these discussions were formally recorded. In this respect, the 2011 two-volume Report drafted by the Constitutional Commission needs to be highlighted here as it documents the wishes and ideas of a sample of 950 randomly selected Icelanders, with some detailed studies of specific constitutional issues and reasoned suggestions for constitutional amendments. As a result, a new generation of Icelanders was able to have their own discussion about the 1944 Constitution, from the adoption of which they had been excluded mainly but not exclusively because of when they were born. Through the 2009–2017 reform process, Icelanders therefore had the opportunity to take ownership of the 1944 Constitution, and to make it theirs. Although this does not necessarily need to result in reforming or replacing the Constitution, the significance for this process from a democratic perspective should not be underestimated.

Icelanders as constitution-makers

The Icelandic constitutional reform will also be remembered for its novel involvement of 'ordinary Icelanders' (to distinguish them from politicians and from experts), a process which was celebrated but which still requires closer analytical and critical discussion. Some mechanisms of participation were familiar and well established, such as the general elections of 2009, 2013, and 2016, which influenced parliament's decisions on the next step of the constitutional reform. Others were totally new mechanisms, namely the 2010 National Forum and the 2011 Constitutional Council.

It is suggested that in this process Icelanders' role as constitution-makers has considerably developed as they were involved, albeit to a various degree, in all stages of the constitution reform, from suggesting issues to be reformed to putting forward some provisions for the 2011 Proposal. This was a new development for Iceland. It is also new in international and comparative terms and raises questions that have yet to be explored more fully at the level of constitutional theory. Icelanders' new role as constitution-makers has tended to be contrasted with that of the established constitution-makers, mostly the institution formally in charge of revising the constitution (i.e. Parliament in Iceland) and a set of experts normally consulted for technical advice. Indeed, the Icelandic reform process and discussion of it have tended to consider these different actors and roles as antagonistic, with the people being presented by some as the only legitimate constitution-makers, while the politicians and the experts were presented as having contested authority and legitimacy. Focus on such antagonism, originating in the deep lack of trust in politicians in Iceland, might, however, not be the most helpful approach to understand and to learn from the innovative Icelandic developments.

The key question might lie elsewhere. That is, it is not about opposing one group of constitution-makers to another, but thinking about how best to combine these different groups and to make the most of their different perspectives on the constitution and of the different knowledge they bring to the discussion. During the Icelandic reform process, much of this happened de facto (or spontaneously) with, for instance, the Constitutional Council of 25 lay drafters consulting with a number of experts and the Parliamentary Constitutional and Supervisory Committee liaising with the Constitutional Council. In addition, it is not completely certain that such a clear division even exists between the various identities of constitution-makers. An 'expert' in constitutional law does not stop being an 'ordinary woman' or 'ordinary man' when drafting her or his expert opinion on technical issues, nor does that individual stop having personal political ideas and views on the subject; similarly, the politician does not stop being an 'ordinary woman' or 'ordinary man,' with all the experience and ideas that this brings. Conversely, the 'ordinary' or lay drafters sitting on the Constitutional Council were perhaps not so 'ordinary,' and in fact a number of experts in fields directly relevant to the drafting were amongst them. The question of what is an 'ordinary Icelander' or 'ordinary person' is not a rhetorical question. To a large extent, the distinctions amongst the various types of constitution-makers were based on the sort of knowledge they are assumed to have (or not to have). Although the question about appropriate sorts of knowledge needs to be approached with caution, it is suggested that, above all, democratic discussion on constitutional reform has to be transparent and inclusive. It is further suggested that a great thing about knowledge is that it can be shared and acquired in a whole range of ways. Indeed, two fundamental questions raised by the Icelandic constitutional reform are about how to educate oneself as a constitution-maker and how to make this education effective and accessible to all.

Democracy, sovereignty, and the *res publica*

Both within and outside Iceland, the constitutional reform has been characterised as an experiment in direct democracy. A greater degree of direct democracy – exemplified by the 2010 National Forum, the Icesave referendums, and the 2012 referendum, and, perhaps above all, the 'crowdsourcing' of the 2011 Proposal – generated much enthusiasm. However, in these discussions the significance of democracy itself, whether direct or representative, has tended to be minimised. It needs to be recalled that, when Iceland's banking sector collapsed in October 2008, the survival of Iceland as a sovereign nation could not be taken for granted, and, deprived of any financial sovereignty, nor could its survival as a democracy. In this context, the adoption of a new constitution or the substantial reform of the 1944 Constitution might not, as such, have led to better or more democracy for Iceland. In fact, if anything can be learned from comparative law, it is quite the opposite. For example, the process of Hungarian constitutional reform started at the same time as Iceland's and in the broadly similar economic and financial context of the 2008 crisis. Although Hungary did adopt a new constitution in 2011, this did not improve Hungarian democracy. At the time of writing, both countries are hit by the Covid 19 pandemic, and both are adopting measures to respond to it. While the Hungarian Prime Minister took on new powers under the Constitution in order to govern by decree for an unlimited period, this sort of approach has not been taken by the Icelandic government. The adoption of a new constitution is therefore, on its own, not a sign of greater democracy.

While the procedures and channels for expressing and representing Icelanders' will and preferences in relation to constitutional reform have been discussed at length, less attention has been spent on discussing what Icelanders wanted to preserve and promote through a reform of their Constitution. Indeed, ascertaining the nature of this common good was one of the greatest difficulties of the reform process, as illustrated by the variable scope of the reform, namely whether partial or total. Nevertheless, some core issues were identified along the way, starting with the list of eight issues to be considered under Article 3 of Act 90/2010 and ending with the three draft articles under the 2016 Constitutional Bill. The constantly changing aim of the constitutional reform did make it difficult to design, let alone navigate, what many have called a road map for completing some reform. Admittedly, this changing agenda was linked to the duration of the reform, as well as to the changes in the political landscape of Iceland during these eight years. This, however, also reflects a deeper level of questioning about the fundamental reason why the constitution of a functioning liberal democracy should be drastically reformed in the twenty-first century, and, if so, what change should be made. Of course, technical improvements are always possible. The issues of how Iceland formally relates to the international community, and of how and to what extent it can or might wish to transfer some of its sovereignty to become part of it, were debated and eventually dropped due to lack of political consensus on these matters. The issue of people's greater involvement in making political, legislative, and constitutional decisions that affect them all was discussed and distilled in the 2016 Constitutional Bill.

Is it possible to innovate beyond these improvements? Historically, the development of Icelandic constitutionalism has been about claiming and securing always greater sovereignty, culminating in the achievement of complete independence from the Kingdom of Denmark in 1944. More generally, the pursuit and safeguard of greater sovereignty and democracy have guided the development of constitutions and constitutionalism. The main question might therefore become about what constitutes the sovereignty of a people and its country in the twenty-first century. In other words, which common good – or *res publica* – is so important to a people that they want to protect it through their supreme law, agreeing on it regardless of all the differences that otherwise separate them? Conversely, what is the public good without which the sovereignty of a people can no longer be exercised? Iceland's 2008 'near-death experience' has demonstrated that a state's ability to control its financial affairs, domestically and on the international stage, is crucial to its political sovereignty. The management of that financial crisis has also demonstrated that this could be successfully done within the existing constitutional framework and with the existing constitutional tools and ordinary legislation. Seen in this light, the other two proposed articles of the 2016 Constitutional Bill on natural resources and on environmental protection may point to different dimensions of sovereignty that have yet to be fully addressed.

As this collection has demonstrated, the Icelandic constitutional reform of 2009 to 2017 requires close analysis in order to identify and grasp its deeper historical, political, and theoretical significance. As the reform process continues, with a refreshed basis since 2018, its outcomes have still to become apparent. It is hoped that this collection contributes to its understanding, not only in terms of Icelandic constitutional specificities but also in broader comparative terms of the theoretical and contextual bases and contingencies of constitutional changes.

Truro, 9 April 2020

Index

Note: page numbers in **bold** indicate tables.

For Product Safety Concerns and Information please contact our EU
representative GPSR@taylorandfrancis.com
Taylor & Francis Verlag GmbH, Kaufingerstraße 24, 80331 München, Germany

www.ingramcontent.com/pod-product-compliance
Ingram Content Group UK Ltd.
Pitfield, Milton Keynes, MK11 3LW, UK
UKHW020014200926
475702UK00014B/1872

* 9 7 8 0 3 6 7 5 5 7 0 8 9 *